CLARK E. MOUSTAKAS is a faculty member of the Merrill-Palmer Institute in Detroit. He is also involved with other colleges and universities in workshops and seminars focusing on creativity and conformity, loneliness and individuality, and human value and learning. His other books include *Loneliness; Loneliness and Love; Learning To Be Free* (with Cereta Perry); *Finding Yourself, Finding Others; The Touch of Loneliness;* and *Creative Life.*

Turning Points

CLARK E. MOUSTAKAS

A SPECTRUM BOOK

PRENTICE-HALL, INC., Englewood Cliffs, New Jersey 07632

Library of Congress Cataloging in Publication Data

Moustakas, Clark E
  Turning points.

  (A Spectrum Book)
  Includes bibliographies.
  1. Personality change.   2. Self-actualization (Psychology)   3. Moustakas, Clark
E.   4. Psychotherapists—Biography.   5. Psychotherapy patients—Cases, clinical
reports, statistics.   I. Title.
BF698.2.M68   158′.1   77-5405
ISBN 0-13-933168-9
ISBN 0-13-933150-6 pbk.

© 1977 by Prentice-Hall, Inc., Englewood Cliffs, New Jersey 07632

A Spectrum Book

10 9 8 7 6 5 4 3 2 1

Printed in the United States of America

Prentice-Hall International, Inc., *London*
Prentice-Hall of Canada, Ltd., *Toronto*
Prentice-Hall of India Private Limited, *New Delhi*
Prentice-Hall of Japan, Inc., *Tokyo*
Prentice-Hall of Southeast Asia Pte, Ltd., *Singapore*
Whitehall Books Limited, *Wellington, New Zealand*

Dedicated To——

The Merrill-Palmer Institute

Major turning point in my life,
love of long standing,
you continue to dazzle me.

Contents

Preface

Turning Points represents a critical period of transition in my own life, a new frontier in discovering fresh roots of my child, adolescent, and adult life. At times in this search a whole new realm of awareness opened amidst anger, fear, despair, joy, or tenderness and sometimes stunning realizations occurred pointing to the meaning of crisis and challenge and of how even devastating experiences of confusion and rejection can be turned into opportunities for self-realization. Above all, once I took the plunge into a transition period, I was lost for awhile, totally absorbed in a process involving dreams, images, and vivid scenes that took me deeply into my own life and into encounters with many other persons. Often the dialogues with others occurred only in my fantasies but sometimes there were direct and actual meetings with persons who held a critical key to my unfolding life or their own.

While *Turning Points* was taking shape I too was intimately coming to know features of my own identity, when and how

these had come into existence and what conditions or crises precipitated them. In concentrating on dimensions of my childhood
identity, and later my adolescent and adult identity, I clearly
began to know my roots and how these have served as significant
forces in my life as a teacher, therapist, and person. I came to
understand what conditions foster healthy growth and what in-
terferes.

For some time I have wanted to be with others who were also
intrigued with their own beginnings, with their own turning
points. I have been exploring with others the emergence of self,
qualities that facilitate or impede, and how they came into existence. I have been concerned with the unity of personal and
professional self in the creation of life with individuals and
families, and in classrooms and psychological centers. I have
witnessed again and again how such a process enables persons to
realize that at bottom each of us is the candle that lights the way,
that taps our sources of energy and power, and that determines
our fate, or each of us snuffs out the candle and remains in
darkness. In every instant, my meditations ultimately resulted in
dramas that compelled me to surrender totally to the root meanings I was seeking. Often these were expressed in poems, in
spontaneous dances, in the creation of stories and myths, in
lucid dialogues, in absorbing dreams, in mysterious forces that
moved me to follow unknown paths or to strike out into completely unfamiliar territory, to risk confrontations with nature,
with myself and with other persons. Although for awhile some
of these turning points held an exaggerated focus and power
over my life, eventually each became fully integrated into the
person I am. I have experienced a growing knowledge of myself
and a heightened confidence to enter into the challenges of
living.

Credits

Many persons joined me along the path of *Turning Points* and shared the journey with me at critical points. In this regard, I especially want to thank Richard Blair, Joseph Herrington, Jr., Barbara Kezur, Leigh Lucart, Kevin MacNeil, Rebecca Naghski, Ronald Ogusky.

I want also to recognize Cereta Perry who offered a supportive, affirming presence as well as events from her own life; Barbara Leonard, Natalie Peterson, Jo Dolley, and Eugene Hoguet who created poems, music, songs, and dialogues that enriched my understanding; Bruce G. Douglass, who assisted with a crucial, final "5-second" transition; and Rik Craig who was willing to explore the mysteries of his own identity and emerged with a strengthened regard for himself. At times during my search Betty Moustakas shared critical shifts in her own life that initiated a chain of associations from my childhood and facilitated this work. Mavis Wolfe lived through the radical shifts and eventually typed the final manuscript.

I am grateful to Mike Usdan of the Merrill-Palmer Institute for his support of this project.

I express my thanks also to the following authors and publishers for reprinting of excerpts from their work:

"Death in the First Person." Anonymous. Published in *The Amer. J. of Nursing*, 1970.

Personal Communication by Richard Blair, The Merrill-Palmer Institute, Detroit, Mich., March 1976.

> *Between Man and Man* by Martin Buber, Tr. by Ronald Gregor Smith. Published by K. Paul, London, 1947.

Love by Leo F. Buscuglia. Published by C. B. Slack, 1972.

> "On Being Number One: Competition in Education" by David N. Campbell. Published by *Phi Delta Kappan*, 1974.

My Mother's House and *Sido* by Colette. Published by Farrar, Straus and Young, Inc., 1953.

"Wanting It All" by A. J. Constance. Published by *The Christian Science Monitor*, 1974.

Personal Communication by Erik Craig, Assumption College, Worcester, Mass., May 1976.

Put Your Mother on the Ceiling by Richard DeMille. Published by Viking Press, 1973.

Hard Times by Charles Dickens. Published by Fawcett Publications, Inc., 1966.

The Poems of Emily Dickinson. Ed. by Martha Dickinson Bianchi and Alfred Leete Hampson. Published by Little, Brown and Co., 1939.

Unpublished Poem by Jo Dolley. The Counseling Center, Bangor, Me., Sept. 1976.

My Little Boy by Carl Ewald. Tr. by Alexander DeMaltos. Published by Charles Scribner's Sons, 1906.

The Experience of Adolescence by Stephen J. Golburgh, Ed. Published by Schenkman Publishing Co., Inc., 1965.

The End of Tyranny by Thomas Hanna. Published by Freeperson Press, 1975.

Culture Against Man by Jules Henry. Published by Random House, Inc., 1963.

Personal Communication by Joseph Herrington, Jr., The Merrill-Palmer Institute, Detroit, Mich., Jan. 1976.

"The Growing Edge." Unpublished Manuscript by Margaret Hoddinott, The Merrill-Palmer Institute, Detroit, Mich., Dec. 1976.

Unpublished Lyrics and Music by Eugene Hoguet. The Counseling Center, Bangor, Me., Sept. 1976.

The Me Nobody Knows by Stephen Joseph. Published by Avon Books, 1969.

Personal Communication by Barbara Kezur, The Merrill-Palmer Institute, Detroit, Mich., March 1976.

If You Meet the Buddha on the Road, Kill Him! by Sheldon Kopp. Published by Science and Behavior Books, Inc., 1972.

The Complete Poems of D. H. Lawrence by D. H. Lawrence. Vol. 1, ed. by Vivian de Sola Pinto and Warren Roberts. Published by Viking Press, 1964.

The Rainbow by D. H. Lawrence. Published by Viking Press, 1961.

The Farther Reaches of Human Nature by A. H. Maslow. Published by Viking Press, 1971.

Human Adaptation: Coping with Life Crises by Rudolf H. Moos, Ed. Published by D. C. Heath, 1976.

Psychotherapy With Children by Clark Moustakas. Published by Harper & Row, 1959.

Personal Communication by Rebecca Naghski. The Merrill-Palmer Institute, Detroit, Mich., March 1976.

Thus Spake Zarathustra by Friedrich Nietzsche. Tr. by R. J. Hollingdale. Published by Penguin Books, 1961.

Personal Communication by Cereta Perry, The Merrill-Palmer Institute, Detroit, Mich., October 1976.

Personal Communication by Natalie Peterson, Bangor, Me., July 1974.

Will Therapy and Truth and Reality by Otto Rank. Tr. by Jessie Taft. Published by Alfred A. Knopf, 1950.

Letters To A Young Poet (Rev. Ed.,) by Rainer Marie Rilke. Published by W. W. Norton & Co., 1954.

What Is Fear? by Jean Rosenbaum and Lutie McAuliffe. Published by Prentice-Hall, Inc., 1972.

The Little Prince by Antoine de Saint-Exupery. Published by Harcourt, Brace & World, 1943.

Journal of A Solitude by May Sarton. Published by W. W. Norton & Co., 1973.

Childhood, Boyhood, and Youth by Leo Tolstoy. Tr. by Alexandra and Sverre Lyngstad. Published by Washington Square Press, 1968.

Artemis To Actaeon by Edith Wharton. Published by Charles Scribner's Sons, 1909.

How People Change by Alan Wheelis. Published by Harper and Row, 1973.

Many Winters by Nancy Wood. Published by Doubleday & Co., Inc., 1974.

Turning Points

For some time now I have been considering turning points in my life, from my first awareness of critical shifts in my growth to the present. I have been completely absorbed in contacting striking features of my self and how they came into existence. What situation, what moment of sorrow or joy, what challenge or crisis awakened me to full awareness and led me, in some significant way, to fashion a new being? How did the features of my identity enable me to recognize and acknowledge myself as a unique person? How did I come to identify self-resources in solving problems and creating a full life? What situation or realization precipitated the journey that made possible the discovery of who I am?

I know now that a central source of my identity goes back to my beginnings, a definite sense of being apart, of hungering, searching for what I never really knew, incredible silences, trancelike states, visions that were not directly connected with everyday people or the known earth, but communions with transcendental spaces and voices. When life offered little expansiveness and vision, I created my own dramas. That quality of imaginative creation is still an important dimension of my identity. Other features have stood out, too—each initiated by important shifts and changes. I have actually felt myself becoming aware of what it means to be human and what it means to be me. During periods of transition, I have come to know my innocence, my way of covering the multitude of destructive happenings that sometimes surrounded me, of finding richness in poverty, and love in loneliness. I have come to know my wild, crazy component, my letting go until everything in me is fully immersed in the moment, freely open, entirely available, in total union with others, with life, with the universe. There is a quality of mystery in me, a movement toward the eerie, the darkness, a fascination with the unknown. There is in me something that is drawn to what is peculiar, different, unfinished, movements into strange caverns and unexplored rooms and into people's worlds that others would not choose or dare to enter. As a child, I recognized my persistent, willful, determined self when I would stay with something long after others had departed or given up. And there were times when I held onto my "No" unyieldingly and asserted my "Yes" with energy, verve, and tenacity. These qualities are still charting my life, still forming my identity—though innocence is sometimes crushed, and imagination and drama are sometimes laughed at, and craziness is met with frozen faces, and mystery frightens or evokes forbidding looks, and my perseverance sometimes frustrates and exhausts. Yet I maintain myself and cherish my identity as fitting and real for me. I have come to recognize within myself determination, fantasy, faithfulness, optimism, love, humility, mystery, sensitivity, persistence, and madness. Again and again, these qualities of my identity emerge and are expressed. Each persists as an important mark of my being, yet each is expressed in unique and varied forms. *changes*

I believe that each person experiences a number of critical turning points that move the person increasingly toward a unique and incomparable selfhood. Turning points are often times of crisis and challenge, times of upheaval that significantly alter the world in which the person lives. Many turning points are connected with family experiences, with beginnings and endings, with discovery, with death and birth, with destruction and creation. Each person within the family and the family as a whole undergo a process involving the expanding of awareness, the emergence of a new identity, and steps toward a new life. The shifts in identity are a continuing process, and like the seasons, they sometimes begin gradually and almost imperceptibly and sometimes with great drama and revolution.

Rudolf H. Moos, from his studies of the impact of crises on psychological growth, has stated:

> A crisis is a relatively short period of disequilibrium in which a person tries to work out new ways of handling a problem through sources of strength in himself and in his environment. His new level of functioning may be more or less healthy than his precrisis pattern. Every crisis presents both an opportunity for psychological growth and a danger of psychological deterioration. During the crisis a person is

more susceptible to influence by others than during periods of stable functioning. Thus, a relatively minor intervention may drastically change the ultimate outcome. Therefore, crises present an unusual opportunity to positively influence coping ability and mental health. The successful mastery of life crises can constitute an important growth experience.(1)

The challenge is for each person to recognize and know these periods of transition, allowing for the flow of life, like the rhythms of breathing in and out; each person must own all that is happening so that life expands in new directions. Failure to recognize, feel, and know these times is like not facing death, shutting it off and thus restricting life, closing resources, and creating fissures within the self that remain inside waiting to burst through to expression in unexpected moments when a word, a facial expression, a color or sound or texture will arouse the dormant feelings and thoughts and send the person reeling to work out what has been suppressed or denied.

The "transition" process was vividly brought before me many years ago when I was being interviewed by a radio commentator who was preparing a program on loneliness and death. I had agreed to talk with Margaret Stone person-to-person but had told her on the phone that I did not interview others nor would I accept being interviewed myself. A few days later we met in my office. Almost immediately she asked a series of questions aimed at identifying me professionally for her audience. Though she had agreed on a spontaneous conversation, to accept whatever direction our meeting took, she was clearly violating our agreement. I interrupted her and told her that I was disappointed that she had not left her interviewing techniques behind, that she had not met me in a fresh way, ready to begin a real relationship. A long pause followed in which we both sat silently. I felt a sadness within me and expressed to Margaret that I would be interested in her own experiences with loneliness and death. Again, there was a long silence and suddenly, all at once, Margaret began to sob. Loud, painful sounds came from her body. When she finally spoke, with a great deal of hesitation she described family scenes that were connected with her mother's death: "I am the oldest in my family. When my mother died, the others assumed I would take care of everything, as I always have. My brothers and sisters left all the arrangements to me and expected me to be available when they needed me. They all leaned on me because I was the strong one. I was coping beautifully. Not once did anyone reach out to me or sense my own inner suffering. I'm weeping now the tears I did not shed at my mother's funeral." Again there was a lengthy silence. Margaret continued her story recounting incidents of mourning and loss when she was expected to stand by and serve members of her family. As she talked she came to be aware of her own alienation from herself. She had felt the shattering nature of her mother's death, yet she had not revealed these feelings to others in the family. For the first time she saw how important it was for her to be the real Margaret Stone, with wishes and hopes and dreams, with feelings and desires and needs—not the Margaret Stone playing the role of oldest sister. Never again would she merely be a tower of strength for others. Never again would she fall into the trap of taking care of others while severely neglecting her own self.

Our scheduled one-hour "interview" had grown into a three-hour session in which I also shared with Margaret an experience of my own in confronting loneliness and death.

My book *Loneliness* was in its final stages when my friend
Eve Winn was dying of cancer.(2) We wrote letters and
poems to each other and lived with each new crisis with the
aid of these art forms until one day I arrived at the hospital
to find that Eve was no longer there. I was informed of her
death by being handed an envelope labeled "In the Event
of My Death." Inside were Eve's birth certificate, her high
school and college diplomas, other vital papers, and all the
poems and letters I had written to her. Until that day with
Margaret, I had not actually accepted the finality of Eve's
death or integrated within me the spirit of Eve that is now
an integral part of my history and a sensitizing force in my
being. I had kept the remnants in that envelope alive by
returning to them as a way of continuing communion with
Eve but I had not internalized death as a continued form
of existence. I had not realized that Eve, as with each of my
important persons who have died, is integrated within me
as an essential part of my being, with me each day in all the
paths of the heart and not merely on special moments of
remembrance and recall.

TRANSITIONS OF CHILDHOOD

In every time of transition one pattern or way of life is
ending, and something new is being born, a new awareness, a determination, a way of being with others.

Here is an example from Golburgh's study reporting a
drastic change in a small child's identity following the entrance of a new baby into her family:

I was three years of age when my brother was born, and I can agree that the birth of a second child may have a detrimental effect upon the first. Looking back, I recall an incident which occurred when I was about four years old. When I heard my mother calling my brother's name, I rushed in from another room and clung to her skirt. She immediately told me to stop being "jealous.". . . This incident stands out above all others that I can readily recall during my preschool years and although I might be wrong, I think the birth of my brother has greatly affected my personality. Before my mother had verbalized my exact feelings that day, I was vaguely aware of something that made me feel as though I had to compete with the new member of the family for attention and affection. . . .

At any rate, my guilt feelings seem to have manifested themselves in a feeling of inferiority which I can recall vividly during my early school years, and less vividly, though I was still aware of it, as I grew older. . . . Even now I have a tendency to fear small closed-in places and this might be an outgrowth of my guilt over feelings of jealousy—the idea that I am going to be punished for feeling this way.(3)

The first major turning point in my life as a child occurred on my first day of entrance into public school when I was severely criticized by teachers. This initiated a process within me that radically altered my world.

I grew up in a Greek family. My mother and father brought with them the roots and patterns of village life where dance and music and food and stories and myths were strong elements, where relationships were open and emotionally expressive, and where freedom and individuality were greatly prized. An argument was a strong emotional battle—with a rapid-fire flurry of words that looked

like a violent exchange but actually ended dramatically
with the opponents profusely embracing and wishing each
other the best of health and a long life. The language was
lyrical, and the Greeks did have a word—often a lengthy
one—for every detail and facet of the world.

My first day of entering school marked an awareness of
my difference, my standing out in an odd way. My primary
language was Greek. I was suddenly thrown into a totally
English-speaking world. My English vocabulary was limited, and though I understood much more than I could
speak, I was teased, belittled, and scorned not only by children but also by my teacher. Because she assumed that my
comprehension was as limited as my spoken vocabulary,
she stunned me with her violent words. She held my parents responsible for my poor language performance. As I
understood almost everything she said, I felt the sting of
her questions and soon became absolutely mute in her
presence. Her criticisms aroused in me a painful search
and struggle to decide who I wanted to be, whether my
Greek life had any value at all. I began seriously to doubt
my Greek life at home and concentrated on learning to
speak English correctly, on killing my own dialect and intonation. Unfortunately, I was successful in removing
much of that unique and special accent of my Greek
tongue. Yet something in me strongly refused to believe
that my parents' language was inferior. I never became
embarrassed by my parents' speech in spite of the criticisms and the standards that my teachers upheld. I re-
tained my love of the sounds, my sense of the tenderness
and the lyyical quality of my native language. When I was
with my parents, spontaneously the Greek words came and
songs broke into the open from deep within me. Their
facial expressions, their use of hands and body were my

own ways coming alive again and still fully there. They spoke with the entire body—everything was alive in their speech—while my public-school training constantly restrained me from using the natural rhythms and melodies of body language.

When I visited Greek villages some years ago, my body came alive with a new energy and I rediscovered the old patterns in lively movements and dialogues. How strange! I was now facing a similar issue in reverse. My principal language as I lived briefly in Greek villages was, of course, English. I struggled to recapture the Greek speech of my early childhood. The response of the villagers was very different from that of my first public-school teachers. These Greeks were now my teachers too, helping me to form the words, encouraging me with receptive eyes and faces and arms. With support from these gentle people, I very definitely was finding my Greek tongue. My speech was mixed with an intonation and dialect that differed markedly from that of the villagers but that did not interfere with our talks nor did they in any way shame or belittle me. They simply welcomed me into their world and accepted with delight my fumbling efforts at communicating in Greek.

What a contrast to my entrance into the American public school where I had been swept into a world of others' standards, where I was determined by others' expectations. For awhile in these American classrooms even my voice was not my own. My teachers fought hard to eliminate all Greek sounds and to standardize my speech as old-fashioned American English. In this first huge transition of my life, I was totally unaware that the issue was not merely one of language but rather one of freedom, the rights of the child, and the authenticity and growth of the self. My identity was at stake, and it was being molded, shaped and patterned by others rather than by the quality, flavor, and satisfaction of my own experience. I am glad my early school-teachers failed to take away the spirit, the rhythm, the caliber, the emphasis and the emotion of my own voice. I am glad I continued to be influenced by the sounds of my Greek home, by my parents' words and songs. What I lost was something of my innocence, of the right to be, and some qualities of my voice. What I gained was an affirmation of the value of my cultural background and a strenthening of the values of my family.

I believe this first day of school represents the beginning of a transformation, the first big step in finding out what it means to be a person in a world that fights for standardization and conformity. Too many parents and teachers are unaware of what this first day means to a child, how an entire world is coming to an end, a single world—good or bad—that is everything. On that first day a second world is opening, and nothing will ever be quite the same again. What a difference to be aware of the revolutionary nature of this change, to feel what it means, and to feel the freedom to express what it means—the fears and dangers, the joys and promises, the hanging on and letting go, the acceptance of one's own timetable for change, and the respect and valuing of one's own orientation.

Here is an example taken from Ewald's *My Little Boy*, of a father who was aware of what it means for a child to leave home for the first time and be surrounded by school pressures a large part of each day.

> He is no longer mine. I have handed him over to society. Hr. Petersen, candidate in letters, Hr. Nielsen, student of theology, and Fröken Hansen, certificated teacher, will

now set their distinguished example before him for five hours daily. He will form himself in their likeness. Their spirit hovers over him at school: he brings it home with him. It overshadows him when he is learning the lessons which they zealously mete out to him. . . .

"Let Petersen and Nielsen and Hansen look out!" I say. "My little boy, for what I care, may take from them all the English and geography and history that he can. But they shall throw no dust in his eyes. I shall keep him awake and we shall have great fun and find them out." (4)

Failure to recognize the impact of beginning school life as a time of crisis and change may have serious consequences for many children in their relationship with parents. A pattern of communication effective in childhood may suddenly cease to work when parents are unaware of the consequences of school life on the inner world of the child.

Karen had been a happy, outgoing, expressive child with comfortable, loving relations with her mother and father. Then suddenly an almost total breakdown of communication occurred with the major conflict settling on Karen's severe dread of school. She began to experience dizziness and nausea on the way to school. She felt she was under surveillance by her teacher, that she was being critically inspected, and that one day she would be attacked. When she tried to talk with her parents, they would not listen to her. They would not permit her to remain at home.

What precipitated her referral to me was the onset of a brain seizure in which Karen lost consciousness in school. Laboratory reports were all negative, and the neurologist concluded that the brain seizure was caused by chronic muscular tensions induced by fear. Karen had undergone a drastic change in feelings, perceptions, and behavior.

The old patterns were no longer effective; a new communication process had to be established.

Here's a sample of the new way in which Karen's father learned to talk with her.

K: Sometimes I purposely fall or hurt myself just to get attention.

F: That's a hard way. Hurting yourself to get sympathy.

K: No, to get attention.

F: That's the hard way.

K: I know a better way.

F: How?

K: By bothering you, pushing you.

F: Yes?

K: Sometimes I even want you to whip me. . . . But when you really hurt me, it stings, I lay there and call you names and feel like whipping you with nine whips.

F: When you're looking for attention, couldn't you just tell us what you want instead of using all these angry ways?

K: I guess I could.

F: What are you looking at out there?

K: I'm looking at the trees. They teach people a lesson.

F: What do they teach you, Karen?

K: The leaves are lips and with their branches they look up to God and God sees them and helps them.(5)

Clearly, in this new pattern of communication, Karen's father is listening, with full human presence and with a concern for knowing Karen in her own world. He is conveying an empathic caring while at the the same time gently pointing to a new path for Karen to consider. It is the first real moment of communion between father and child as they begin to find each other again in real ways.

In a remarkable series of childhood incidents, my friend Cereta Perry awakened to new attitudes with reference to herself, events in which dialogues with her mother and father had altered her sense of self and offered her values that would remain with her as sources of strength all of her life. This, briefly, is her story of the three major turning points of her childhood.

A major turning point in my childhood occurred during my fourth year of life. I remember distinctly how it was for me to enter into dialogues with my mother. It was during personal crises, in dialogues with my mother, that I learned to exercise the power of my being. On two separate occasions especially significant interactions took place between us. They still stand out as I consider the turning points of my childhood.

In the first situation, I come into the kitchen leaving a playmate outside. I tell my mother (in a somewhat hurt manner): "Mama, Emma called me black."

My mother responds in a clear, definite, supportive way: "Yes, you are black. I'm black and I'm proud of it."

I remember the feeling then of really being okay with what I had first perceived as an affront.

In the second situation (in the same year, as a 4-year-old preschooler), I come into the house quite upset:

"Mama, Jennie said I was stupid." This time my mother's response was: "This is a free country. People can say what they want to say. That does not mean that whatever they say is true. You must not let people's words tell you what you know is not true."

The message which I took from my mother's responses was: "Pay no attention to a person's words when you know that what they are saying is untrue. Listen to your own words!"

These two situations were powerful influences in the formation of my identity. They provided me with the foundation to accept who I am, to give myself the power to value myself, and to deny others power over me. As I combine these two incidents, a crucial change occurred in me, a new strength, and presence to be who I am and to value myself. I believe my mother moved me early in the direction of self-determination. It is currently a center of my identity—the capacity to make choices and to determine my own fate.

A second critical incident of my childhood that changed my entire life involved a confrontation with my dad when I was 8 years old. I viewed my dad as a very powerful man who was quite authoritarian. His slightest wish for many people in his world was a command. He seemed to give orders and people obeyed without questioning him. I often thought quietly that I wanted to change this situation. One day I set out to change it for me.

My dad came home from work, and while my mother was preparing dinner, he announced that we were going to play a game until dinner was ready. The "we" included six children and him. I did not feel like playing, so I did not accept the invitation. He repeated his announcement that everybody would play. I held fast that I did not intend to join him. He then said angrily, "Cereta, you go upstairs and no dinner for you!"

I remember skipping upstairs and saying gleefully but quietly "he couldn't make me play; he couldn't make me play." I felt I had won my battle. This incident represents for me a strong beginning of self-assertion. It has served me all of my life. Strangely enough, this was also the major turning point in my relationship with my father. It cemented a bond between us, we remained good friends, the love and respect abided.

The death of my father when I was 11 years old was a tragic event. Our nuclear family now included my mother and nine children whose ages ranged from 1 to 16 years of age. My mother was faced with a huge responsibility, and she summoned all of her resources to meet it. She made no special demands on us. Her spirit influenced me to help as much as possible to lighten her load. I was the oldest girl (there were two older brothers), and I began to assume some of the responsibilities of homemaking and child care. This was not imposed but was clearly my choice. I was aware of my decision and realized a sense of fulfillment in being a responsible person. This sense of responsibility is still a central feature. From time to time, I focus on "who am I." Always three words come clearly to mind: self-determined, assertive, and responsible.(6)

As I am engaged in this process of returning to critical transitions of childhood, all at once I am overwhelmed with a time in my life that might have devastated me and sent me into a spiraling darkness. I had lost touch with this time through the years but now as I am focusing on turning points in my life I look inward to that time. I am becoming aware of its indelible traces, of feelings still alive within me. I am turning back to my life with Ron.

From the first day we met in the third grade we immediately came under the magical spell of friendship. Each morning we walked together to school, taking a different path through backwoods and back roads, along passageways that we created. Each morning we embarked on an unknown adventure, taking turns in mapping the route. Always, there was surprise, laughter, and the wonder of really noticing everthing along the way. Every morning opened a new life.

Ron lived about halfway between my home and our school. We would start our journey each morning from his home, and as we walked or skipped or ran we discovered the beauty of new and fresh awakenings.

I lived in a family and in a neighborhood of economic poverty but was not aware in any way of being poor. Ron came from a middle-income family, a difference that I had not noticed until our fifth-grade teacher, Miss Janis, made it the central issue. From the way she looked at me and spoke when she called my name, I felt her instant rejection of me. From the moment I entered her classroom my presence antagonized her. She was appalled by the way I dressed, by my "poverty," and obviously troubled by my friendship with Ron. I can still hear her whispering to me, "Ron's parents don't want you around anymore. Don't go where you're not wanted! Stick to your own kind." I had no idea what she meant but the tone of her voice, and the intensity of her feeling frightened me. From that day on, she belittled me frequently. She attempted to shame me and was continually arranging ways to defeat me. Somehow I did not take in her words and feelings. I did not permit her to crush me. I continued to learn in spite of her attacks. And I did not pull away from Ron. He dismissed her, saying, "She's crazy. Don't bother with her!" Something inside, some source of life, enabled me to continue—in a way not to be touched by her cruelty. In silence and in quiet meditations, I continued to find my center, to trust in it, and to be on good terms with it. But now as I see Miss Janis before me I feel inside the pain of her rejection of me, the hurt that my very presence would arouse such negative feelings. I believe I transcended her harsh judgments and her caustic labeling of me, yet at this moment I am aware that somewhere deep inside I am weeping for myself and for all children who know the pain of rejection. That pain is still there. Perhaps some trace of it always will be.

The experience with Miss Janis was my first of total rejection, my first realization that simply my being me was repugnant to somebody. I found solace in meditation, in quiet daydreams, and in imaginative scenes. I came to see for the first time the importance of silence, the value of staying in touch with and affirming my own self.

I came to know myself in a different way, to realize that I am a free person, that I create and choose my perceptions of me, that my thoughts and feelings are my own. Miss Janis did not succeed in destroying my friendship with Ron, but we avoided being together in her presence. For the first time I saw how poverty could arouse prejudice, how in itself it could become the basis for rejection. That awareness sensitized me to a compassionate respect for all differences. It also evoked in me a resolve to stay on my own path, to follow my own senses, to find a way to keep alive my joy. Regardless of how others might want to stifle or stop me. I was determined to keep on singing.

In the mood of this realization of my own value I am reminded of this poem of Nancy Wood:

> Hold on to what is good
>> even if it is
> a handful of earth.
>
> Hold on to what you believe
>> even if it is
> a tree which stands by itself.
>
> Hold on to what you must do
>> even if it is
> a long way from here.
>
> Hold on to life even when
>> it is easier to let go.(7)

Recently a friend shared with me her reflections on returning to a forbidden place of her childhood. In the process she had found a new belief in herself and a hope and vision of the future. The forbidden place was a pond that was lonely and peaceful, with sunlight that danced on the water, a place for walking into mud and feeling its lovely coolness. "Oh, how I love this place." she exclaimed. "How happy I am here—but I'm not supposed to play near the pond." And with this expresssion, Natalie engaged herself in a dialogue, her adult self speaking to her child self:

Adult:	You're beautiful!
Child:	No I'm not! I shouldn't be here and I'm getting my clothes all dirty!
Adult:	But it really doesn't matter—you're happy here.
Child:	Yes, but my mother gets so angry with me if I don't. . . .
Adult:	It's hard when others don't understand.
Child:	I get so confused! What *they* want me to be is not what *I* want to be!
Adult:	And?
Child:	And they're grown up and they should know more than I do.
Adult:	Perhaps, but they aren't *you.* Someday perhaps you'll come to trust yourself.
Child:	No. My self is unpredictable and unknown!
Adult:	But you're beautiful!
Child:	Even when I'm not good? Even when I get my clothes dirty? Even when I don't do what I'm supposed to?
Adult:	Yes—always in all ways!
Child:	Oh, how I want to believe you—to believe in myself! Maybe—just maybe.(8)

The discovery of a young boy that he does not have a father, does not know his father, and probably never will is a shocking awareness. For Rik, it created a long search, a hunger to find someone who would be his father. All his life he searched for this man, reached out for him, and now at last he came to realize that his father did not exist and never would. Returning to the first moment of awareness of his difference from others to this major turning point in his life, Rik experienced a period of sustained pain and anguish, and then gradually he found a way out, the miracle of being his own father, giving himself what would not come from any other man. His poem conveys his search and the realization that came from it.

> Reaching up for that
>   big hand, that man's hand
>   firm, warm, gentle
> Me in my baggy, black shorts.
>   The clean, straight legs of a child
>   soft yet solid
>   and planted firmly on the ground
> Reaching up for that
>   big hand, that man's hand
>   I remember. . . it's not there
>   it never was.
>
> Funny. . .
>   that I keep reaching
>   I keep seeking
>   not for that big hand, that man's hand
>   anymore
>   but for all the things I once
>   secretly feared only it could give me.
> I know differently now
>   I have learned how to ask for what
>   I want, need, wish for
>   And I have learned how to give myself
>   what others will not offer.
> Oh, yes, I recognize this doesn't erase the memory
>   of that hand that was never there
> And I *do* see that I don't always succeed in
>   my new found ways
>   but at least I know now
>   some things I didn't before.

And I do
   keep reaching
   I keep seeking
And I've come to believe that I will
   as long as I still have breath.
I do reach
   for ultimate experiences and ways of being
   for joy, hope, friendship and love.
And I do seek
   for passion, beauty, truth
   for the wonders and miracles that
      come with each new day.

That, old man, mysterious man
   is your gift to me
   you have made me a reacher,
      a seeker
      for eternity.(9)

Every person in some ways experiences a sense of loss, the power of illness and crisis, the facing of unknown threats to health and potential dangers to life. Every person has also faced the awareness of a shocking truth, when one world is ending and another is beginning. The cycles of living and dying and being reborn, the death of one self and the birth of another self, are part of every period of transition. When there is awareness of what is happening in life and a willingness to live, to face the challenges openly, to struggle with them, and move forward, turbulent shifts in identity and self-transformations occur. Personal breakthroughs erupt that lead to new awareness and marked changes.

I invite you the reader to consider the turning points or periods of transition in your childhood, the times of personal breakthrough in awareness or significant discovery Make a list of these. Select one major turning point and create a story or dialogue with yourself or some other person, or perhaps a poem or a scene, that depicts the range of feelings, the mood, and the impact of this transition. It may be a time of joy or sorrow, a time of realization. Include in your expression the visual and auditory, and the sense of touch to convey the voice and texture and tone of your experience. Go off to a quiet place and be in touch with this time in your life. Take time in solitude and allow it to flow from your memory, your images, and the shadows, dreams, and voices of your own child life. Be silent for awhile, and then find someone you love to share what you have created.

TRANSITIONS OF ADOLESCENCE

Patterns that are effective at one point in family living may fail to make contact between parent and child at another point. In the transition from childhood to adolescence a new world of perception, feeling, interest, and activity is opening. The old ways of parents being with children no longer work as children move into the more expanded world of adolescence. In my own family, with each child, I found the shift represented a major transition as a result of the impact of school, peers, music, sports, and other pulls from the outside world. I found that to continue to relate fully and effectively, with each person becoming a teen-ager, I had to develop new patterns of communication, new interests, and new ways of being. I found myself fully engaged in discovering the excitement of rock music and jazz where classical music had previously been central; in knowing about and participating in sports and games, where solitary activities had been my natural choice; in learning about automobiles and boats, where walking and running had been my preferred mode of moving from one place to another. In all of these what was required was a new language, a persistence and dedication to keep alive relationships that had been open, spontaneous, and creative in childhood. Thus, for me the adolescence of "my" children at home awakened new avenues of life and new paths of interest and activity. To be part of these worlds, I had to shift what I listened to, how I listened, and where I might expand to make the necessary connections. To my surprise I really began to enjoy these new interests. They became integral for me. And, there were many times when I initiated and pointed to new possibilities in these areas, when I became the creator of new life, rather than simply adopting or taking on the preferences, tastes, and styles of "my" teen-agers.

From my experiences as a child and family therapist it has become clear to me that in many families child-parent relations have been on a positive level but a significant breakdown occurs when parents attempt to use the same patterns of communicating and relating during the marked shifts that occur in adolescence.

Adolescence in itself is a critical period of transition. The world of childhood will never be the same. In significant ways that world has ended, and a new life is shaping and forming. Sometimes the shift is gradual, but often dramatic changes occur that drastically alter a person's identity and the way that a person is known by others. It is easy at these times for parents to lose touch, through faulty awareness, through habits that no longer work, through failing to notice and actually see and feel and hear what is happening.

Even when there is an awareness of a crucial transition occurring between children and parents, it does not always move toward understanding, accommodation, and new commitment. Sometimes the barriers and resistances become firm, resentments accumulate, alienation and divisiveness set in. A high school senior describes the incidents of early adolescence that totally changed his identity and his relationship with his father.

> Up until the ninth grade, father and I were very close. We used to work together building things and remodeling the house. I used to help him with his job and we got along fine, until I asked him to go fishing or play ball. He kept telling me sports were a waste of time and I should spend more time working around the house. My favorite sport was football, and my sophomore year I made the first string. This was a great achievement for me and I was very happy about it. All my friends and neighbors cheered me on, but I felt very lonely because father hardly ever went to watch me play. I became more withdrawn from him and at times it seemed I didn't know him. . . . I went off by myself and thought about things and analyzed my problems by myself. I began to show resentment toward father for his lack of interest in school activities.
>
> I showed this resentment by doing the opposite of what he told me to do. He wanted me to work, so I decided to loaf. He wanted me to join the service, so I decided to go to college. Everything he planned for me I did just the opposite.(10)

Leo Tolstoy has written about his own transition from childhood to adolescence.(11) The major shift was in the form of a conviction that "man's purpose in life is to strive toward moral perfection." For him there was a sense of urgency that marked the years of his youth, a sense of how much time he had already wasted and a determination to apply this conviction to all phases of his life and "the firm intention never to be false" to it. The challenge of the transition to adolescence is to keep on growing in new and vital ways and to relate these shifts to an emerging identity and selfhood, to risk again and again what it means to be human, to be a unique person, to be related, to live creatively.

Perhaps the most dramatic unfolding is in connection with new love relationships. The relationship of love when it permeates one's being changes the entire world. Especially in adolescence is this totality experienced, where love often becomes everything. Nothing remains the same. Colors, textures, sounds, food, all of life takes on a fresh, dazzling beginning. Rooms brighten and move; energy skyrockets. All at once the world is a beautiful place, and there is a sense of being able to do what one wants, a sense of great freedom, of visions and dreams. Nothing is impossible, when the spark of love fills life. All of one's senses come alive in the glory of the revelation, the glory of the fullness of intense feelings, in this new, completely enthralling relationship, in the limitless boundaries and sensations that love creates. The breakup of such a relationship sometimes moves young people to the other extreme, of despair and illness, of darkness, the dimming of energy and of life itself.

When Beckie returned to her adolescent years, to the major turning point of that period of her life, what awakened most emphatically was the end of her first love relationship. Beckie's decision to end it plagued her for some time but she was also aware that a new feature of her identity had emerged—for the first time she knew the feeling of being entirely alone in making a crucial decision and in taking responsibility for it. She created this poem to portray the impact of this relationship as a critical transition in her life.

Just one look at my first love
Was enough to light my eyes like Christmas candles
We danced with innocence and carefree youth
It was the world of a football star and homecoming queen.

But the outside world called and the train screamed
Our tears melted together as one and we stood naked at
    future's door
We had lost our magic as the dragon Puff had lost his mighty
    roar.

My dreams were crushed
My heart became a battleground
    and the battles that ensued were bloody and deadly.

On a September night alone
No one near me who knew me
I decided to close my heart
    and turn my back on my first and only love
I wrapped my warm and tender heart so vulnerable and lov-
    ing,
    still bleeding and hurting, in a hard armour
I protected it as it was near ready to die.
Brutal act, selfish act
My battle was now within myself
To ward off those feelings of guilt and feelings of love.(12)

In one of our meetings, my friend Rich Blair shared the impact of the death of his father as a critical turning point in his life. I had asked him to share with me a special time in his life when a new feature of his identity had come into being. He chose the crisis of death in his early adolescence as the first time that he realized he had powers within himself to stay on a path of determination and courage and to overcome adversity, to act valiantly in the face of extreme fear. That quality of courage is something he knows and depends upon today.

While in an isolated setting, he learned that his father was dying. To reach his father he had to pass through a thick forest on a dark, stormy night. Immediately he started his journey. As he considered this transition in his life, I suggested that he go off alone and choose some art form to recreate the experience. He came back with this—his *Mourning Song*:

> The Sky it is dense and wet
> And the road slick with Rain
> I will push through these torrents and
>   tree limbs severed from their trunk
> I will strain to make my way through the DARKNESS.
> Through the rolling fog from the meadows
>   which chokes my senses, closing me off.
>
> The Lump in my throat swells with every mile
> Every mile an eternity of DARKNESS,
> Every mile more lonely than the last
> Relief comes only from the sometimes flash
>   of lightning shooting down before me,
> illuminating for a moment the next winding stretch
> I am to navigate.
>
> The Sky it is weeping for you
> And I am coming, I am making my way through
>   the DARKNESS.
> It is hard for me to see you,
> For the sky it is weeping, my father.
> Every mile an eternity of DARKNESS,
> Every mile more lonely than the last.
>
> The Sky it is dense and wet
> And I am weeping, my father.(13)

Of course, there are many other situations that precipitate significant change in adolescence, beyond the opening of intense interests and absorbing activity, beyond love relationships and death in the family. Certainly alcoholism and drugs often initiate pronounced changes in personality and character, and in behavior—often complete transformations in which the whole world changes.

When I consider the times of my own adolescence I become aware of new relationships as being central turning points, relationships that brought awakenings and crises, that markedly altered my sense of self. It was during these years that I realized that I knew how to listen and feel into the heart of a person's communication. During this time young people often approached me with family problems or other concerns. Mostly, I was aware of simply being fully present and in the process noticing a lifting of the heaviness or the fear or the anger. It was almost a magical thing, the change that would occur in the other person's tensions and agitations by my human presence and caring. I began to perceive myself as being able to enter into the heart of a person's struggle and assist in its resolution. When I consider this as a turning point of my adolescence, I am aware now of the profound change this brought into my life. I had found a way of being with others that I valued, a way that others recognized, and one that fitted my own sense of self, a way that offered a resource for the expression of my potentials. I was able to put into life processes that had been part of me from my beginning, a deep absorption with life, an energy for focusing and imagining, and a dedication to examining and searching with eyes and ears and heart.

One other shift of my adolescence is still a central feature of my adult life—the discovery of movement and of myself in movement, letting everything go and entering totally, freely into dance. One day when my life was dark and I was feeling the barrenness of my world, I turned on a radio and suddenly began to move with the music. To my surprise the heaviness almost immediately lifted, I relaxed completely. My body jumped and leaped and soared and floated. It was a time of total immersion in dance, a trance-like state of absolute levity. I let go completely and was once more fully at home with myself—the rhythms, the euphoric movements, the touch of earth and sky, the utter breathlessness of pure joy. I had cut the heaviness that surrounded me, and I knew what it was to be crazy, to let go, to be completely free.

In adolescence, I often entered into acute identity experiences. For a while they colored my entire existence. Everything revolved around the person or issue or crisis. All of my life became centered in the one specific occurrence and I remained with the process until I experienced a sense of fulfillment or completion, until everything in me had been released, expressed, communicated, in all the nuances and variations. When I reached that point once more I would feel a wholeness and a unity in my life. I also recognized a new feature of my identity, standing out in a way that told me I would never again be quite the same person. Something crucial had happened, leading to new strength, conviction, determination, awareness, knowing.

When I consider the different types of situations in my adolescence that evoked unborn components in me and urged me into an active, creating, centering way of life that took over for a time, I recognize seven situations that precipitate acute identity experiences.

1. Crises that are connected with chronic illness, dying, death, or any major loss.

2. *Opposition* that challenges and provokes me into new

searching, centering, awareness, action, into becoming, in some way, a different person. I have grown a new self many times through difference and conflict with others.

3. Peak experiences that often occur unexpectedly, spontaneously, in which there is total immersion, such as my experience in Greek villages, with the return of my original language, the rediscovery of Greek foods, music, sounds, textures, and patterns that reawakened and created anew my joy in movement and dance. The Greek component is now definite as a feature of my identity.

4. An atmosphere or climate that nourishes, supports and invites has at times precipitated an entirely new process, started me on a special journey into knowing myself and actualizing new components of my identity. Such an atmosphere enabled me to come to know myself as a writer, when throughout high school and college English courses I wrote only on demand, only when required. Now I do not write on demand but only as a natural or spontaneous desire to express and to communicate; then I know my writing is alive, in an immediate and full sense.

5. Completely immersing myself in a single interest, theme, or question and searching heuristically (subjectively, in terms of self-awareness and self-dialogue) to discover the meaning of my life as an individual and my life with others, whether children and families in therapy, my involvement with children and teachers in schools, or the patterns of communicating and relating with friends and within my family. I now see myself as a humanistic researcher facing life's issues, problems, and challenges, and in the process changing as a person and as a professional worker, altering my identity.

6. A significant relationship that is suddenly shattered or broken through a new awareness of the true nature of

the relationship, or through a critical misunderstanding or an incident that arouses suspicion and mistrust, or through any realization or change that tosses the value of the relationship into a sea of doubt. This precipitates a long search and struggle that generally leads to a radical change in the relationship and a new dimension of identity.

7. Relationships that affirm my identity, extend and expand the self and enable me to realize new strengths, new resources, new ways of being alone and with others. Such relations open new potentials and add new features of identity.

Through my support and affirmation of Sara, for example, she moved from a concept of herself as non-assertive to one of being assertive. In our talks, she learned to say "Yes" and "No," without feeling guilt and remorse, and she learned to express herself clearly and definitely —in contrast to my first meetings with her in which even the most provocative situations failed to move her to be assertive. Thus she had often been manipulated, exploited, and used.

In one incident, her dentist told her she needed to have her upper molars ground to have a more even bite. She did not respond at all though she did not want to submit herself to this treatment. She was satisfied and comfortable with her way of masticating. She finally was able to tell him that she would rather not have her teeth ground, but the dentist proceeded anyway to do one molar. He told her he'd finish next time she came in. She remained silent, but fuming. She maintained this anger until we talked. In our interchange she began to find power within herself and, at the end of our talk, she declared, "Next time he starts I'll scream at him, 'Stop, what are you doing to me. I told you

I don't want my molars ground!" ' This was the beginning of Sara's assertiveness and her belief in herself as an assertive person, as a real dimension of her identity that enabled her to declare herself, to state her position, and to take a stand when she felt others impinging on her rights.

Once more, go off alone and find your place for communion and self-dialogue. Be aware of your growing into adolescence and make a list of the transitions at that time that influenced your identity and the specific awarenesses or qualities of your being that came into existence. Choose one of these for deeper exploration and create in words and images the revolution and the unfolding that occurred. Find someone important in your life and share what you have created to portray a feature of your identity that came into existence in your adolescence and still vitally reflects the person you are.

TRANSITIONS OF ADULTHOOD

When there is awareness of what is happening in life and a willingness to face the challenges openly, to struggle with them, and move forward, turbulent shifts in identity and self occur. During adult years, personal breakthroughs erupt that lead to new awareness and marked changes. Each transition leads to new discoveries; as new perceptions are formed, the way a person feels and lives is significantly altered. Each new upheaval, each new truth alters patterns of life. Transitions are inherent in growth; throughout life there are continual openings, chances for new beginnings, realizations of new ways of being.

Major adult turning points include the departure from

school life and entrance into the world of work, bringing a drastic change in the people of everyday life, and a whole new set of interests, activities, standards, and values; marriage with the radical changes in autonomy and all facets of living; the birth of children that critically changes the patterns of communicating and relating in the family, threatens stability of the marriage, shifts the nature of activities, and creates a crisis in the identity of the persons; divorce with its pain, upheaval, and altering of the entire structure of life; retirement and aging with the continuity of an active, productive, valued life being threatened and with the constant battle to remain alive and fully functioning, often in the face of rejection, humiliation, and violence.

For me, some of the most crucial challenges of identity in adulthood occurred in intimate relationships, in the struggle to remain autonomous and free; to keep faith with the serious and the crazy; to find absolute and enduring values, to maintain trust in the face of hypocrisy and distortion; to continue to believe in the essential goodness of life in the presence of betrayal, manipulation, and broken promises; to maintain an authentic stance and a responsible presence whatever else might be in process of transforming.

I return to one of these disturbing relationships that significantly altered my sense of who I am, a relationship that ultimately tapped from within me new sources of energy, life, and creation that I would call upon when confronted with interference, denial, and rejection. In this relationship, I need not succumb to distortion and betrayal, I need not be defeated or crushed by trickery or deceit, but could hold onto what is real for me. Painfully, I learned a way of turning inward, finding strength and continuing to believe in myself, in others, and in life itself. In the writing of this experience I feel the courage to continue to be. This portrayal of the experience in written form helped to reaffirm this strength and courage.

Yes, Tom, you really spoke to me as we stood alone. For the first time, you looked directly at me and your eyes offered hope. From somewhere you were saying that you accepted me, that our differences did not matter anymore, that in basic values we were in harmony. Slowly, you took me into your world, and all at once I believed you. I trusted you with my entire being. It was a moment that went beyond all the other moments as we spoke with each other, and suddenly all the suffering and the doubt were gone. The terrible labels that you had put on me washed away. Remember, how I stayed with you, how I listened, even when you shrieked at me and branded me a liar. With all my energies, I met you on that angry ground when you challenged everything in me, everything I wrote, when you used my words against me, taking pages from my *Loneliness* book and twisting the meaning of the passages until I felt my spirit moving from life to death and did not know if I could continue to remain with you in the utter pain of darkness and despair.

Now in the new moment in the darkening shadows, somehow, unbelievably, everything had changed. You spoke of your own agony of becoming aware of the injustice and I believed you. I opened myself to your life, to you. I entered and found your warm gentle smile. It was near the end, and like good food that offers life and energy after a long fast we came alive together. At last, I experienced you as a real person, a friend coming into the light from darkness. I believed in you, in myself, in the sources of the human power to effect drastic change when there is good will, in spite of all the misunderstandings, the angry reading, and the laughter and mimicry that followed my stories, my words and phrases. We walked out together into the radiant setting sun. And we sang songs of joy, for we had come all the way around, moved from extremes, and found a true beginning with each other.

That friendship, that beauty, that euphoria stayed with me only with the disappearing sun for in the dawn ahead your letter came and shook the ground I walked on. You told me it was all part of the grand scheme, part of your drama, you denied everything with harsh and condemning words. With each of your words, I died a little inside. My mind was whirling and dazed. I paused to catch my breath. I was gone now, lost, alone, no more feeling, knowing, being, everything covered and disguised. I fell into a bleak and painful emptiness, abandoned, criticized for being and for not being. I did not see your words anymore, I stopped hearing voices or sounds of any kind, living in that deep, dark numbness that overtook me. My senses died that day, and for a while I walked without hope, a living death.

Nothing, no one moved me or touched me anymore. I no longer trusted the sounds of my own voice or my footsteps on the path. Nor did I trust the other voices that surrounded me. Nothing seemed to matter now. It was a lost and endless time.

And then suddenly the whole world changed again. You came along. You entered my door and jarred me, Holly, with your gentle, quiet waiting. I tried to hide from you, to become invisible, but you stood in my path, determined not to let me go, not to allow me to disappear. You waited in silence and when that silence became unbearable you appealed to me to speak. For a long time there were no words that would come and then from who knows where the broken cry of my voice: "I—don't—trust—anyone—anymore!" You fell forward screaming, throwing your arms around me. You shattered every cell in my body. We fell holding each other, and your tears washed over me like piercing arrows. You wakened me from the dead, wakened me with the realization that I was robbing you of innocence, of unqualified loving, of acceptance, of me. To say I didn't trust *you* was like shearing you into a thousand splinters. I knew then that that trust that had always been there for you was still alive. Your cry broke through my paralysis with a power that restored my faith. Never again would that trust be doubted, shattered, or denied. We held each other in a long, long silence. Suddenly our eyes sparkled, we had found each other again. With joy and laughter we walked out to wait for the new day. For me there was the realization that raw feelings in the extremes of dejection and euphoria would mark my being forever, to intertwine and blend with life. No matter how devastating a future moment might be, my faith would always shine in me, in people, in life. It would never again be silenced. It would live forever strong. There have been direct and indirect betrayals since that day, but my faith has continued unshaken—even when I have felt the sting of violent criticism and rejection.

Another major turning point of my life occurred when I was faced with the serious problem of whether to agree to major heart surgery that might restore my daughter to health or might result in her death. The urgency of making this critical decision plunged me deeply into feeling utterly alone as I deliberately cut myself off from the guidance or compassion of others.

At this time I discovered the roots of my own loneliness.

This realization took me back to those early adolescent years when I felt apart from others, often wandering alone into the woods, watching the movement of clouds and creating and imagining patterns and visions that often ended in stories that I spoke or wrote to myself, and back to many other moments that flashed before me—the violation of trust, the discovery of the lie, the betrayal of friendship, the end of innocence.

The awareness of myself as a solitary and lonely person was a revelation that changed my life. I would no longer avoid or deny or run away from myself or push myself into activities but would remain open to the process and feel the reality of life as it is being lived, accepting the darkness and the light, the levity and the serious nature of communicating and relating. This penetrating discovery of my own isolated existence opened a flood of feeling within me—a more poignant awareness of the evening sun fading into oblivion, the urge to live honestly, the full determination to make my life of consequence, the intimate sense of nature and people, a deeper contact with myself. I began to see life in more vibrant forms than I had ever experienced before. I came to seek and to know each member of my family in a profound awakening of a whole range of feelings—excitement, exuberance, joy, and sorrow—laughing with my entire self in moments of wonder and joy and weeping without restraint in the face of broken communications, illness, tragedy, and death. Each aspect of my life took on a color, a distinctiveness and vividness that was entirely new for me. Something extremely powerful had taken root, and I came to know myself in a fuller sense and to commit myself to the truth of my life with others. I learned that I could grow, that I could find a path, in lonely silence. The discovery of myself as a lonely person, the realization of the value of solitude, would serve as a resource in times of conflict and stress and in times of repetition and stagnation. I knew that in lonely meditation new ideas and images and feelings would be created in poetry and dialogue and narrative and that I would talk more freely to myself and eventually find the way to renewal of life with others and to deeper ties and relationships. This was *the* major transition of my adult life and permeated everything else, my marriage, my family, friendships, work—my entire life.

A friend recently shared the significant turning point of her adult life, her discovery of herself as a free person, as a person with power to meet the unknown and to create something lively and good for herself. She describes her first experience in leaving home to travel to a foreign country:

> I can't believe I'm really doing this! Myself, a small town girl here on this big ship with all these people jabbering away in a language I can't understand.
>
> Ugh! Another wave breaks. I feel so sick. I think I'm crazy to be here. How did I ever get so brave—maybe it's not bravery but stupidity. Yet, here I am, all alone, depending only on myself and beginning to know that I really can depend on myself—and even like it. I kind of like this ship and being all by myself. I'm free to do whatever I want and just pay attention to me. And I don't even feel lonely. How freeing it is to be able to enjoy an experience by myself—to not need someone to be with me to share it.

Those plump Greek women over there chattering and
    fussing over their kids
The dark, dark night, full of sways and turns and jerks
The lightly lit corridors crammed with people
The smell of cooking and spices
And always an unceasing melody of voices.

I soak it all in and I feel full!

I can't get away from the rocking and feeling sick. I'm excited but my body is fighting this. Maybe I will get a bed for awhile. Wow, that feels better—to be horizontal instead of vertical and to drift into a dreamy, image-filled sleep.

I awake again to the human sounds all around me—all of it is a blur because no words stand out. The sun flows into the windows, those funny, round windows. And I can see the vague outline of land. It looks so inviting, all those mountains and the wildness of it all.

Then it hits me! I don't even know where to go when I climb off of the boat. Which direction is the village, how will I get there, how will I communicate with people? Where will I stay?

I don't feel so brave now—last night I had the security of the boat. Now I am really on my own—how shall I manage—I so wish I were home—I'm afraid and all alone and I don't trust myself to take good care of me right now. I drift off of the ship, moving with the mass of people, and I lug my backpack up onto the bus that everyone is trying to get onto. I don't know where this bus is going but most people are taking it—I expect it goes somewhere.

I begin to feel more settled and I consider my resources. How can I help myself right now? I look around me on the stuffed bus and I become aware of a couple, one with red hair and the other wearing safari shorts. They don't look Greek, in fact they look Australian. Jerk! The bus stops and the couple gets off and I dash to follow them.

> Drinking retsina
> laughing and talking,
> long wanderings through the village and sign
>   language chats with people,
> climbing through the gorge of Samaria,
> and long, refreshing swims in the sea, Andrew and I
> trying to teach Judy to swim.

I did manage on my own, which means that I had the

power to make things happen in my travels. It didn't mean I always had to be alone or independent. I could initiate contact with people or remain alone—it's up to me and I can choose and I can make my life exciting and adventurous.

> And I can do it under my own steam
> What freedom opens up to me!
> I can determine my entire life! (14)

The dawning of a friendship in adult years is often the turning point in opening new dimensions of the self. Sources of life and energy that have never been tapped before are suddenly touched off. The world expands and deepens and something inside each person waiting to be born is given full assent. It is as though these two persons have been hungering from childhood to discover a friend who will release a whole untapped reservoir of poetic communication and creative expression. And now they have found each other! A light beams, the energy flows freely and a brand new dance comes into being. The relationship initiates a process of creation and life where anything is possible, a friendship filled with mystery, a sense of the wonder of life, and a constant vibrancy.

Such a friendship was the major turning point for Jo and Gene. As a way of portraying the magic of their friendship and the creative sparks it evoked, as a way of recognizing and honoring their feelings for one another, they created poems and songs—a completely new medium for each of them. They were absolutely at home with each other, and experienced a tranquility as soon as they came together. They spoke to each other in lyrics and melodies. These songs depict the fulfilling nature of their companionship.(15, 16)

Who - are   you?   and who - am   I ?   We're two grown up

chil - dren   just learning to   cry, and to   hurt   and be

sad   and be   mad when we   need to; or to   laugh   and to

play   and   be   gay   when we   want to.

1   There's no need to be   phon - ey   or play games, dearest
2   Oh —   can you be-   lieve it ?   We've come such a long
3   So I Know who you   are   now   and you know who I

friend —   and we'll ne - ver be   lone - ly
way —   to al - low our- selves   feel - ings
am —   We're two   grown up   chil - dren

or feel   separate a - gain ———— Now that the boy/child in-
and be   able   to   say: "I am   not ———————— al- ways
in this   family   of   man, and   what — we share with you

side   me   who was   al -   ways   a -
strong, ———   and I'm   not ——— al-   ways
now   friends   and ——— hope you find   to   be

Jo's Song

His old folk song was a sing-ing rhyme, and he
sang it soft in the dark night time, and his smile was
warm, and his song was sweet, so I curled myself up be-side his feet.

2. I laid my head up against his knee, then somewhere deep
   down inside of me, a little girl that I used to know,
   woke up and came and found him so.

3. And his loving eyes pushed away the gloom, in the quiet dark
   of a late night room, and the little girl with the smiling face,
   who had looked so long for a being place,

4. Just lay her head up against his breast and in his strong arms
   found a place to rest, with her dark brown hair hanging soft and long
   she went to sleep hearing his heart's song.

5. And his singing rhyme just kept going on, on and on,
   it kept going on, in the soft dark night, 'til it came the dawn
   his singing rhyme just kept going on.

I would like to close this search with you for the significant turning points and transitions in forming identity and selfhood with the spirit, mood, and message that this poem of Nancy Wood conveys.

A long time I have lived with you
And now we must be going
Separately to be together.
Perhaps I shall be the wind
To blur your smooth waters
So that you do not see your face too much.
Perhaps I shall be the star
To guide your uncertain wings
So that you have direction in the night.
Perhaps I shall be the fire
To separate your thoughts
So that you do not give up.
Perhaps I shall be the rain
To open up the earth
So that your seed may fall.
Perhaps I shall be the snow
To let your blossoms sleep
So that you may bloom in spring.
Perhaps I shall be the stream
To play a song on the rock
So that you are not alone.
Perhaps I shall be a new mountain
So that you always have a home.(17)

I invite you once more to find a place for exploring turning points in your adult years. This time take writing and drawing materials with you, or other materials you may want to use to discover creatively the major transitions of your adult life. Be alone and get into touch with these times. Make a list of your turning points—people and places and situations that initiated a significant awakening, a change in identity, a new world coming to be. Consider perhaps a major relationship that ended, marriage that ended in divorce, a love relationship that was terminated, a significant friendship that altered its nature in terms of trust and intimacy.

Create an expression of one turning point in your life. Then find someone close to you with whom you would want to share the dawning of this dimension of who you are. The expression may be through art, through poetry or narrative, or verbally through a relating of your expanded awareness, the nature and range of your feelings, and a pointed sense of your own identity.

REFERENCES

1. MOOS, RUDOLF H., Ed. *Human Adaptation: Coping with Life Crises.* Lexington, Mass.: D. C. Heath, 1976, p. 13.

2. MOUSTAKAS, CLARK. *Loneliness.* Englewood Cliffs, N.J.: Prentice-Hall, 1961.

3. GOLBURGH, STEPHEN J., Ed. *The Experience of Adolescence.* Cambridge, Mass.: Schenkman Publishing Co., Inc., 1965, pp. 111-112.

4. EWALD, CARL. *My Little Boy.* Tr. by Alexander DeMaltos. New York: Charles Scribner's Sons, 1906.

5. MOUSTAKAS, CLARK. *Who Will Listen?* New York: Ballantine Books, 1975, pp. 35-36.

6. PERRY, CERETA, Personal Communication, October, 1976.

7. WOOD, NANCY. *Many Winters.* Garden City, New York: Doubleday & Co., Inc., 1974, p. 78. Text copyright © 1974 by Nancy Wood. Reprinted by permission of Doubleday & Co., Inc.

8. PETERSON, NATALIE. Personal Communication, July, 1974.

9. CRAIG, ERIK. Personal Communication, May, 1976.

10. GOLBURGH, STEPHEN J., Ed. *Ibid,* p. 35.

11. TOLSTOY, LEO. *Childhood, Boyhood, and Youth.* Tr. by Alexandra and Sverre Lyngstad. New York: Washington Square Press, 1968.

12. NAGHSKI, BECKIE. Personal Communication. March, 1976.

13. BLAIR, RICHARD. Personal Communication. March, 1976.

14. KEZUR, BARBARA. Personal Communication. March, 1976.

15. HOGUET, GENE, Unpublished Song. The Counseling Center, Bangor, Maine, September, 1976.

16. DOLLEY, JO. Unpublished Song. The Counseling Center, Bangor, Maine, September, 1976.

17. WOOD, NANCY. *Many Winters.* Garden City, New York: Doubleday & Co., Inc., 1974, p. 71. Text copyright © 1974 by Nancy Wood, Reprinted by permission of Doubleday & Co., Inc.

The Gift Of Self

When I focus on the gift of self, what comes immediately into my awareness is the power that each person possesses to create images and fantasies and dreams —wishes, feelings, and ideas, the inner source of life that each person holds to create a continuing, growing selfhood.

This power to create life was the crucial force of my own childhood. At the center of my world was a capacity for invention, a way of being that offered intrigue, variety and adventure. My special place for fantasies and dreams was a window ledge that was cold in the winter and hot in the summer. For this reason no one else in my family chose to be there. But, for me, it was the perfect setting from which

I could let my imagination flow outward to the forests, the canals, and the rivers and inward to new pathways of hope and vision. At the center of these creations was an awareness and a life of my own—a life that absorbed me completely in stories and poems and songs. Kneeling from my ledge I created paintings with clouds. Images and symbols moved in and out in continually shifting designs. Through my window I imagined dialogues with exciting people —walks in the park, rides to the beach, excursions into the country. Sometimes these scenes of my imagination were forerunners to actual conversations, to exciting picnics and carnivals, to swimming places in summer and skating rinks in winter. I encountered people of all ages in my neighborhood who spoke of child life in myths and stories, in memories and reflections. Always, these imaginative creations were filled with intense scenes, vivid colors, and dramatic adventures. In imagination was the beginning awareness of a potential, a promise of new life. The capacity to create imaginatively from my own self, to create a life before it was lived, awakened in me a desire to venture forward, out into the world to express my fantasies and dreams, to find a way of actualizing my imaginative dramas and thus to enrich my world. Visual and auditory dreams broke into the static routines of everyday life and brought excitement, intensity, and feeling.

The fantasies of my imagination were often ways of talking to myself, ways of gaining courage to face an unknown threat, to meet obstacles, to brace myself to deal with difficult situations. They were times of harnessing my energies and making possible the tapping of what was available in me for new activities and new experiences. These imaginative creations were often the catalysts that enabled me to meet difficult challenges and find my own

way. The imaginative powers of my childhood have persisted. I affirm Nietzsche's portrayal of the child's
strength:

> But tell me, my brothers, what can the child do that even
> the lion cannot. . . .
> The child is innocence and forgetfulness, a new begin-
> ning, a sport, a self-propelling wheel, a first motion, sa-
> cred YES,
> Yes, a sacred Yes is needed, my brothers, for the sport of
> creation: the spirit now wills *its own* will, the spirit sundered
> from the world now wins *its own* world.(1)

This gift of self to create through imagination and fantasy, in a special place, is very much part of my current life.
Today, although there are places of communion everywhere I travel, my office is the special setting for visualiz-
ing the unfolding dramas of my life. In my office I experience a tranquil feeling that almost instantly creates a mood
within me, to ruminate and to dream. My office is a sanctuary that invites imaginative pursuits and provides a
complete feeling of being at home. I am quietly alone,
thoroughly absorbed in the silent creations of the heart,
realizing fully the precious feeling for life.

This poem of Nancy Wood, growing out of her life with
the Navaho Indians, speaks for me:

> The rock strengthens me.
> The river rushing through me
> Cleanses
> Insists
> That I keep moving toward
> A distant light
> A quiet place
> Where I can be
> Continuous

> And in rhythm with
> The song of summer
> That you have given me.(2)

When I am wanting to create a new life with a person that I have not met before, I begin with the creation of my own mood or atmosphere. I believe that self-growth begins this way—with an attitude, a receptiveness, a willingness to go wide open, to see what there is, to hear all that is available, to feel and know what is in me and before me. So, I begin by finding a comfortable place, my own special place where I am entirely at home with me. Sometimes I light a candle to recognize this is a special occasion. I sit quietly until I am breathing peacefully, until I am at rest. I let the silence speak to me, and I speak to it. I steep myself in this silence to be aware of the wonder of life, the mystery of each new relationship, the joy of creating life with another human being. I become aware of the meeting as something unique in itself. In this way I am getting ready for the new journey. The silent, meditative life is preparation for communion with others, a way of recognizing each meeting as its own thing, a way of creating a mood that is receptive, welcoming, alive.

Everything is direct, open, spontaneous, immediately available. Nothing is derived, explained, aalyzed. The human climate is alive with an immediate invitation to talk, to remain silent, to move, a dance of life—never a secondary process of observing, questioning, directing, interpreting.

My words speak to immediate moments, to root meanings, to felt awarenesses. And my silence is a way of awaiting new life—in absolute quiet, affirmative and supportive, a positive invitation, an inviting glance, a reassuring expression. And thus we begin in a way that encourages and supports individuality and freedom.

In the same way that I create a mood to pave the way to life with others, I create an atmosphere for my own growth when I meditate in silence, in a special place that welcomes me, a room that invites me and feels my presence and rejoices in it.

And then anything is possible.

My window ledge was alive with spirits that welcomed me. My office contains these friendly spirits—so while some people are talking to their plants to create healthy life I talk to my walls and ceiling and floor, to my pictures, and paintings, to my songs and poems, to the powers within me.

The environment of my office is vital to me in a way that my eyes and ears are vital to me for there I am in touch with vibrations and sources of life that exist nowhere else in the world. My office is my source of wonder, of dreaming, of being immersed fully in whatever is current, alive, forceful within and without. This process of imagining and creating I learned in my childhood. It has served me well throughout my life. It is still with me.

This, then, is my first message to you. Find your own places of creation, and let your imagination flow freely. In the classroom, create a climate that encourages images and dreams and permits their expression in paintings, in storytelling, in conversations, in dramas, in dances. The natural tendency of children to enter into trancelike states too often has been tampered with and so impaired that creations of the imagination may not come easily. It may be necessary to assist the process by creating a mood and bringing in resources that will nourish and support the fancies of children. The *Hard Times* adults of Dickens' day are still with us.(3) The Thomas Gradgrinds of the world are still condemning flowers on walls as unnatural and horses on carpets as irresponsible. Do you remember: Fact! Fact! Fact! You are to be in all things regularized and governed.

Rarely are the most significant learnings based on fact alone. Rarely do facts determine our choices or govern our actions. An example of Carl Rogers in a paper on cognitive and affective components of learning comes to my mind. In backing out of his garage he had crushed a flower that he had lovingly nourished to growth and greatly prized. The facts of distance and length and width of which he was well aware made no imprint, but the emotional depth of the experience of seeing his precious flower damaged made his learning of perception and judgment a permanent thing.

To overcome the teachings of an ordinary reality and a production-oriented society, it is often essential to create compelling powers in the classroom, forces that are strong enough to overcome past conditioning and reawaken in children their own dreams and fantasies and ruminations. Drama and dancing, literature and the arts are resources for inspiring awareness and initiating new beginnings. Books like *Put Your Mother on the Ceiling*(4), *Left-Handed Teaching*(5), and *Wishes, Lies, and Dreams*(6) offer strong, pervasive examples, ways of exercising natural capacities for imaginative expression.

I especially like this dramatic way of saying it all at once, from *The Me Nobody Knows*:

> I think that women are the greatest thing that happen to man because men and women have the power to produce. And that all I got to say.(7)

Creating a mood that is powerful and pervasive is often the first step to the life of fantasy and imagination. The mood I want to create is the towering feeling of not being able to wait, of wanting to experience something fully, instantly, completely, all at once, rather than in the gradual way that most things come our way as adults. Here's an example of what I mean.

I construct elaborate protective devices against the world, but from time to time someone comes along who walks right through these defenses, utterly unaware of them. When this happens, I feel vulnerable and open. There is a mingling of fear and happiness, because I realize that I am on the brink of something new and unpredictable, something that will find its own shape, form, and texture.

As I wait in the silence of the unfurling relationship, there is a taut anticipation of something expansive, regenerative, and extravagant. There is a sense of being on the brink of life—on the edge—where amazing things can happen, where there may be hurt and rejection, but where there may also be sharing and affection and growing toward the light.

It is a dangerous and delightful time, this newness, this waiting. Is there any miracle on earth to compare with that of discovering a new friend, or of having that friend discover you? So much is at stake, but I will and do, risk everything to give a promising relationship a chance. . . .

One of my most agonizing weaknesses: to want it all, all at once— complete expression, complete knowledge, complete relationship, complete understanding. To have life, at every moment, on the fullest, grandest possible scale. I am impatient with fragments and halves, with tidbits, hints and nuances. And yet (I tell myself, again, and again), there is built into the nature of things a necessity for stages, subtlety, and degrees-of-things. A flower unfolds petal by petal, a river meanders its way along to the sea, the sunrise

comes quietly, with shadings of wonder, and love grows
from grace to grace.

I know this, I do know it, I do. Intellectually, I understand and accept the necessity for orderly progression in all
these things. And yet the emotional me *still* wants all at
once the fullness, the dazzling totality.(8)

Consider something in your current life. What would it
be like to have that all at once—the hope, the vision, the
dream, the dazzling totality?

Another way of my childhood that offered me an an-
choring, a significant connection, a vibrancy and zest for
life was the development of special rites in relation to other
people, in relation to myself and to nature. Rituals created
in me desires and hopes and special feelings. I remember
as a child how I began each day with an early awakening
that involved certain specific meditations and movements,
rubbing of eyes, turnings of my body, and listening to the
sounds outside my window. These rituals gave each morning a unique meaning. Often I focused on a single event or
person that was to be the source of excitement. As a child,
my thoughts and feelings sometimes turned toward my
friend Ron and what the day might hold for us. Though
the anticipation was never the same as the reality, the process of engaging in early-morning rituals was as rich and
wonderful as the actual events that occurred. Being with
Ron was like the touch of the morning breeze that would
build with remarkable energy and exuberance. I am reminded of my daily journey to his house and the path we
took together to our school. It was always the same—the
way we greeted each other, the games we played, the trees
and houses we met along the way. We shared a life that was
always alive, vital, and fresh, yet each day contained the
same rituals that grew out of our unique way of being

together. I now know that rituals protect a person in a way
of life, enabling him to live in his or her own world of
magic, to own that world and to find love and joy in it.
Rituals make a relationship alive with special flavors and
textures, that belong only to the persons involved and
safeguard them from being invaded by standards and expectations of others. Rituals are like a secret code, secret
messages created and expressed only for I and Thou.

One of my most magnificent experiences in therapy was
with Barbara, who since early childhood had been
humiliated, taunted, and called hunchback because of a
severe spinal curvature. My usual ways of beginning were
ineffective with her. She sat absolutely still, numb to nearly
all of my comments or my silence. One day she arrived
looking weary and unhappy. She asked for a cup of tea.
From this simple request a process of therapy was initiated
that resembled a Japanese tea ceremony—a series of rituals each containing a special and unique meaning, beginning with the quiet preparations and culminating in a slow,
savoring drinking of the tea. At these times, when Barbara
spoke her words were not edgy or agitated. She spoke of
different aspects of her life and described the people she
encountered during the week. On the whole she lived as a
recluse and rarely left her home. Our weekly meetings
became the pivotal point of her life. In mysterious ways
our rituals awakened her, and she began having regular
contacts with a number of adults in her neighborhood.

The tea ceremony was the center of our world. I often
sat with her, entranced as she gently spoke of the events of
the week, presenting them in the form of a gazette but
without the usual linking words and connecting phrases.
In simple, poignant expressions she spoke of current and
pending activities. She had not lost touch with tenderness

or with simple values; each event was like a treasure for her; she enjoyed each act, each vision of reality, noticing a blade of grass, watching the movement of a cloud, savoring the flavor and warmth of her growing communion with others. When she came, my office was alive with spirits. Strange moods filled the atmosphere. I experienced a distinct feeling of joy, a kind of levity and light, a sense of tranquility no matter how frustrating or busy my life had been. Our rituals brought me a feeling of peace and contentment. Sometimes we engaged in private reverie or we meditated. Something in her presence touched off something unique in me, and a feeling of wonder was created. Our meeting room became a sanctuary.

As I have indicated, most of our life together revolved around the tea ceremony, but our meetings always ended with a music experience. Experimental surgery aimed at correcting her back deformity had caused extensive brain damage and had destroyed most of Barbara's cognitive skills; she no longer wrote or spoke in the usual ways; she did not read in ordinary ways; most of her communications were atypical and could be understood and appreciated only through the meaning of rituals. I came to value these vivid words and shorthand expressions; just one of her words was a sudden bursting through to life. Everything from her past had been altered or severed, but somehow she had maintained her connection with music. One day following the tea ceremony, Barbara expressed a desire to play for me. From this time, with each visit she brought a different selection, usually of classical music, and we always ended each session in the same way. Often groups of birds congregated outside the window and chirped in harmony. As Barbara played exquisitely, we entered into a kind of trance, and when the music was finished, we walked lightly, with renewed energy and optimism.(9)

Perhaps "rituals" are all that so-called mentally ill patients have left of their own inventiveness and creativity. The damage of trying to destroy the rituals of hospital patients is like taking everything away—to rock-bottom nothingness.

Many years ago I discovered that I was not alone in holding onto the innocent magic of my childhood—the belief that rituals were essential in the creation of reality and that my happiness and life depended on them. I have learned that every genuine relationship contains rituals and patterns that distinguish the way that people come to know one another and the unique ways of being together.

> "It would have been better to come back at the same hour," said the fox. "If, for example, you come at four o'clock in the afternoon, then at three o'clock I shall begin to be happy. I shall feel happier and happier as the hour advances. At four o'clock, I shall already be worrying and jumping about. I shall show you how happy I am! But if you come at just any time, I shall never know at what hour my heart is to be ready to greet you. . . . One must observe the proper rites. . . ."
>
> "What is a rite?" asked the little prince.
>
> "Those also are actions too often neglected," said the fox. "They are what makes one day different from other days, one hour from other hours."(10)

Rituals enhance the relationship and turn it into a special and private affair. The value of rituals is spontaneously realized by many parents who establish special ways of relating with their children—rituals that contain a unique flavor no matter how often they are repeated or how crazy they may appear to others. Rituals can continue to hold a particular meaning into adulthood and old age, thereby adding zest to meetings with significant others.

Consider for a few minutes the rituals that are important in one of your relationships. What are these rituals? Permit yourself to feel the wonder and magic of rituals. Now play a selection of music. When the music stops, share the rituals of one relationship with a person near you.

I am very much aware that not all childhoods awaken feelings of the magic and joy of life, of the miracle of play and of the spirit and drama of human experience. For many persons, childhood represents a time of terror, of upheaval, a time of crisis and anguish and rejection. Some persons are able to recall only destructive turning points, crushing times, feelings of rejection and inferiority, inhuman denials carried forward into adolescence and adult life, to mark an identity with features that are limiting, demeaning, and death-like. These are childhoods that were ruined by indifference and by cruelty. They are fully documented in the vast literature on emotional disturbance, conflict, and upheaval, in autobiographies and in the clinical reports of patients in mental hospitals and in intensive psychotherapy.

It is my belief that however disastrous the events of childhood, there continues within each person a source of life, a kind of magic energy that is fresh, naive, childlike. That core of the child within the person can never be totally destroyed. It lies within waiting to be activated in some new time of crisis or challenge or in some new time of loving invitation. The unexpressed gifts of childhood are always with us. It is in that spirit that I continue this journey, to invite, awaken, inspire.

I wish now to move to another quality of my childhood that is still very much part of my current life—a way of immersing myself totally and completely in some interest or activity so that nothing else exists for a while. At such times, I want to be entirely free to pursue my interest and to stay with it to a point of fulfillment. As a child, I often watched the movement of ants, grasshoppers, worms, and other insects for hours and hours. When called I felt that I was being jarred out of a trance or dream state. At a later time, I became interested in detective stories. Every morning I hurried to the local library and plunged into reading every author of mysteries from A to Z.

When I first read *Crime and Punishment*, my life revolved around Dostoevsky until I had read his *Notes* and all his novels. I had a similar experience with Thomas Wolfe, D. H. Lawrence, and Hermann Hesse; still later, others captured my mind and heart totally, like John Dewey, Carl Rogers, Abe Maslow, and most of the Existential poets, novelists, dramatists, and philosophers. As a child, when I first began to swim and later to ice skate for a while every day, these activities were the most important thing in my life. When I collected leaves, I searched everywhere to identify, know, and relate to the trees of my neighborhood. It was the same with puzzles, construction and model kits, and games. I would stay with the one central attraction until I fully integrated it into my life and was ready to move on. That quality of being fully alive with one all-embracing theme totally absorbed my energies and resources when I engaged in a study of loneliness. All my waking hours and many restless nights were centered in thoughts and feelings of loneliness—my conversations, songs, music, readings—every facet of my world revolved around becoming more fully aware, recognizing and knowing loneliness in all its creative powers and its destructive affects.

I remember that when my son, Steve, was in the fourth grade his world revolved around the sun and satellites and planets. He appeared to be hypnotized while exploring the heavens, badgering his mother and me for references, maps, telescopes, trips to science museums and the planetarium, until he clearly understood the solar system to his satisfaction. He immersed himself totally in this interest, stretching his capacities, going beyond all the ordinary limits of involvement, and exhausting his energies —until he experienced a sense of fulfillment, a letting go, and was ready to move on. And move on, he did—to coins, to rocks and stones, to rock music and blues, to girls, to mechanics and cars. New horizons continually opened, and when they did everything else was secondary, everything else receded. I have greatly enjoyed that force and energy, the fascination, the wonder, the fullness of a life totally committed to inquiry and pursuit of what is essential, or what can only come from direct participation, from primary processes, from inside the heart of a person.

The spirit of my message is contained in this passage from a letter of Rilke:

> ... be patient toward all that is unsolved in your heart and ... try to love the *questions themselves* like locked rooms. ... Do not now seek the answers which cannot be given you because you would not be able to live them. And the point is, to live everything. *Live* the questions now. Perhaps you will then gradually, without noticing it, live along some distant day into the answer.(11)

If learning is to tap the sources of life that are within each of us then we must be free to remain with that which truly provokes and captivates us, that which enlists our involvement and collaboration. Strange as it may appear, no person remains with a single interest forever. Having satisfied curiosity and experienced a sense of fulfillment, the individual ventures into life with eagerness for new adventure, new knowledge, and new experience—a new spark.

Edith Wharton expresses it this way:

> There are two ways
>   of spreading light; to be
> The candle or
>   the mirror that reflects it.(12)

As a child I always wanted to be the candle to light my own destiny rather than mirroring the reflections of others' ideas and achievements. I still want to be that light.

Being the candle that spreads light was very much a characteristic of Barry. In hours of play therapy, between his wars against the animals and his attacks on his baby sister, Barry concentrated on painting. As the year unfolded it was not uncommon to hear Barry singing, mixing paints and creating unusual designs with bright, vivid colors. When he was immersed in painting, he was quiet, deliberate, diligent in his efforts. At these times it was like a miracle to see the dynamo that was Barry become peaceful. Painting definitely provided a release for Barry; in it he found his medium for self-expression and relationship. At these times the tight, drawn face and the darting suspicious eyes changed radically as Barry was in a trance of relaxation and joy. His paintings were a serious and profound expression of his being. More than anything else the painting process subdued his wild furies. Several times during the course of therapy, he announced "When I grow up I'm going to be an artist. I am an artist." In his paintings, he put his whole being, and he valued what he created in all its dimensions. Once he started he was in a world of his own, and he wanted no one to interrupt him.

As he painted, Barry came to understand and to know himself. He discovered what he could do and who he could be, and this discovery brought a special meaning into his world. Through creation in art Barry became someone. For a while, the tension and agitation disappeared, and the gentle side of Barry flourished.

The spirit that is Barry is still very much with me—the tough and tender feelings; the hard, dominant leader and the soft and cooperative partner; the pounding, incessant willfulness and the receptive, enabling person, the loud, noisy, and boisterous dynamo, and the serene and peaceful artist. I lived with him fully in all of these dimensions, and my own spirit rose on that final day when he left with confidence and with pride, carrying his last creation. I hope, Barry, no man will ever cause that fire in you to dim, that the artist in you flourishes and grows, and that now that you have taken a major step in that direction you will continue to be who you are.(13)

In his paintings, Barry willed to be himself and to become fully a unique person both in his sorrow and in his joy. His joy especially was passionate and shook everything in him vividly alive. This poem of Emily Dickinson speaks to me of Barry's way:

> I CAN wade grief,
> Whole pools of it,—
> I'm used to that.
> But the least push of joy
> Breaks up my feet,
> And I tip—drunken.(14)

For a few minutes you be the candle and immerse yourself completely in some situation. What would it be like to let go totally with all your energy, spirit, and feeling? Are you able to respect this process and support it with people who are central in your world?

I would like to move to a dimension of my childhood that remains as a striking component of my current life —that special gift of the self to continue to change and shift and grow, through taking risks, through venturing into the unknown, through the mystery that is present in all of life. Sometimes I venture into dark rooms, into prisons and dungeons where terror is carefully concealed or where rage lurks. I have stayed while others might have walked away. I have continued to believe without any evidence whatsoever, only a blind persistence and trust, that new life would come and bring with it laughter and joy and love.

Many of the people who are important to me today are individuals I have come to know through daring to respond to cracks in a door, daring to enter and remain. While others might have been pushed away, I persisted, challenged by the mystery, the risks, filled with the spectre of radical, intense, strange unfoldings.

As a child I was fascinated by the deviant person, the odd one, the individual who stood out because of peculiar actions and interests. My fascination was not that of morbid curiosity but rather of wonder and of the promise of mystery, of entering a totally different kind of relationship without any notion of what would be coming, of the sometimes bizarre worlds I discovered, frightening, compelling, exciting, joyous. I was always aroused by spirits and ghosts and witches, not experiencing them as frightening but as unknown forces that attracted me, that had a life of their own and stories to relate from which I could learn.

I ventured forward into the mystery of the person, wanting to encounter that person fully where others would not pursue, to know what was most sacred, most feared or most loved, to evoke the rare or uncommon in myself and others, to share the unique and different. In many paths I have traveled, when danger threatened me I still moved forward and faced the challenge of the unknown. Ultimately, the mystery unfolded and brought wonder, delight, and amazing discovery. Or, it unfolded in painful realizations. In either case these were lessons of life that added drama and spark to what might easily have been a limited, mechanical, and dull existence. Everything in life has potential for meaning and value as long as there is mystery. I have taken the path of the unknown, enjoying the bypaths, the roads not traveled on; I still enjoy losing my way; I am still fascinated by the sudden, strange turns of my journey. I firmly believe that mystery and the unknown move children to discovery, to pursuit, to exertion beyond ordinary limits. When I listen fully to the spontaneous urgings of children or of myself I recognize the desire to explore new worlds, energy and life that radiate from intangible spaces, messages that come from the sun and the other planets, strange connections and associations with symbols and shapes, attractions and warnings, that have no logical or rational basis, whisperings of the universe—the leaves, the rain, moving shadows, the voices of night. Excursions into the unknown still fascinate me. I value what I am able to learn from the unusual, what I am able to feel from sources I am unable to locate or verify. I believe that life is impoverished when we dare not venture where we have not been before, when we are taught to fear moving toward the undisclosed, when we remain always safely in the light.

A passage from D. H. Lawrence's *The Rainbow* powerfully expresses my own valuing of mystery:

> That which she was, positively, was dark and unre-
> vealed, it could not come forth. . . . Yet all the time, within
> the darkness she had been aware of points of light, like the
> eyes of wild beasts, gleaming, penetrating, vanishing. . . .
> She could see the glimmer of dark movement just out of
> range, she saw the eyes of the wild beast gleaming from the
> darkness, watching the vanity of the camp fire and the
> sleepers; she felt the strange, foolish vanity of the camp,
> which said "Beyond our light and our order there is no-
> thing," turning their faces always inward towards the sink-
> ing fire of illuminating consciousness. . . . and the System
> of Righteousness, ignoring always the vast darkness that
> wheeled round about, with half-revealed shapes lurking on
> the edge.
>   Yea, and no man dared even throw a firebrand into the
> darkness. For if he did he was jeered to death by the others,
> who cried "Fool, antisocial knave, why would you disturb
> us with bogeys? There *is* no darkness. We move and live
> and have our being within the light, and unto us is given
> the eternal light of knowledge, we comprise and com-
> prehend the innermost core and issue of knowledge. Fool
> and knave, how dare you belittle us with the darkness?"(15)

What is crucial is most often hidden; it takes courage to
face what has not been lived before. Opportunities for
engaging mystery are everywhere, within and without. I
believe that we must recognize and encourage these qualities of daring, fascination, wonder, curiosity, that we must
enter worlds of the bizarre, the unusual, the unique to
bring sense and balance to the ordinary realities that we
believe represent sanity and health. The unpredictable
and unknown are still the best sources of renewal, awakening, vitality and drama in living. New life is created

through mystery, moving out into the world, wide open to explore and discover and create new paths to one's own self, to others, to awareness and to the knowledge of nature and life. As a child, I was attracted to what was dark and unrevealed. Wherever I found the glimmerings of mystery I moved. For where there was mystery there was always life, always a strange opening ahead, always active and compelling. There is a mystery about me that will always remain. I seek to encounter that mystery in each of life's ventures. It keeps me alive, with sensual acuity and presence. I respect the unfinished, the undeclared, the unspoken in myself and in others; I move toward the darkness and awaken to new visions. At this moment I feel its presence and await the new path that is open to me, to you.

I will close this chapter with one final dimension of my childhood. When I was a child, there were always games to create, places to discover, hidden clues that would move me forward. There were hunts of various kinds—eggs in secret places and coins in special loaves of bread. Surprise was a vital component of my life with others. It allowed for private ways, and brought on laughter and joy and crazy antics. Some of the major events of my life since childhood have been connected with surprise—discovering the amazing world of children in therapy and the beauty of a relationship in a private place, getting married, the birth of babies, finding myself a writer, rediscovering my Greek childhood and suddenly being able to understand and speak my forgotten language in remote Greek villages, journeying on unknown mountain paths with Greek gypsies, being invited to travel to far-away places, and discovering people all over the world who have become part of my extended family. I am still stunned by the wonder of opening a door and finding a long-lost friend. The surprise element of a gift has always been as important to me as the gift itself. I delight in surprising and in being surprised. How strange that many of us have lost touch with the joy of surprise, with creating moments of surprise with our friends and families, with the fresh, lighthearted gaiety of the startling and the unexpected. For me, surprise has always been part of the innocence of childhood. As a grown-up, it remains as a value, as something uplifting, something positively astonishing.

Being open to surprise I often find myself in unexpected places, having no sense of how I got there but suddenly becoming aware of the new environment, the trees and roads and houses and people; each turn on the road brings additional discoveries and I am encouraged to explore further.

Being open to the unexpected often means a willingness to shift directions and to travel in unknown places. Whether surprise is spontaneous or planned, it deepens and extends relationships, it brings a levity that balances the heavy and often serious nature of human affairs.

Create a plan with specific intentions and actions regarding one person in your world; then share this plan with someone nearby as a first step in bringing the surprise out into the open. You may also wish to consider a list of surprises that might be incorporated into your classroom, your professional work, or your personal life.

REFERENCES

1. NIETZSCHE, FRIEDRICH. *Thus Spake Zarathustra*. Tr. by R. J. Hollingdale. Baltimore: Penguin Books, 1961, p. 55.

2. WOOD, NANCY. *Many Winters*. Garden City, N. Y.: Doubleday & Co., Inc., 1974, p. 47. Text copyright © 1974 by Nancy Wood. Reprinted by permission of Doubleday & Co., Inc.
3. DICKENS, CHARLES. *Hard Times*. Greenwich, Conn.: Fawcett Publications, Inc., 1966.
4. DEMILLE, RICHARD. *Put Your Mother on The Ceiling*. New York: The Viking Press, 1973.
5. CASTILLO, GLORIA A. *Left-Handed Teaching*. New York: Praeger, 1974.
6. KOCH, KENNETH. *Wishes, Lies, and Dreams*. New York: Chelsea House Publishers, 1970.
7. JOSEPH, STEPHEN. *The Me Nobody Knows*. New York: Avon Books, 1969, p. 91.
8. CONSTANCE, A. J. "Wanting It All." *The Christian Science Monitor*, Nov. 25, 1974. Reprinted by permission from The Christian Science Monitor © 1974 The Christian Science Publishing Society. All rights reserved.
9. MOUSTAKAS, CLARK. *Who Will Listen?* New York: Ballantine Books, 1975, pp. 137-139.
10. SAINT-EXUPERY, ANTOINE DE. *The Little Prince*. New York: Harcourt, Brace & World, Inc., 1943, pp. 67-68.
11. RILKE, RAINER MARIA. *Letters to A Young Poet*. Rev. ed. New York: W.W. Norton & Co., 1954, p. 35.
12. WHARTON, EDITH. *Artemis To Actaeon*. New York: Charles Scribner's Sons, 1909, p. 23.
13. MOUSTAKAS, CLARK. *Who Will Listen?* New York: Ballantine, 1975, pp. 56-57.
14. DICKINSON, EMILY. *The Poems of Emily Dickinson*. Ed. by Martha Dickinson Bianchi and Alfred Leete Hampson. Boston: Little, Brown and Company, 1939, p. 19.
15. LAWRENCE, D. H. *The Rainbow*. New York: The Viking Press, 1961, pp. 437-438.

Creating, Willing, And Being

In the last chapter, I explored five key features of my childhood as they related to celebrations, features that were alive then and with me still today, crucial in distinguishing me as someone with definite markings, in contrast to being a vague, amorphous, and generalized man. I shared these features because they opened something of great value for me and I believe they offer a potential to find and enjoy the child that is in each of us. These features were: first, a capacity for creation, invention, fantasy, and imagination; next, the development of special rites and rituals, and their place in all of my significant relationships; also, a way of immersing myself totally and completely in some interest or activity so that for a while nothing else exists; another feature is my attraction to the unknown, to mystery, a movement toward the peculiar, the radical, strange, deviant, or undisclosed; and, finally, the component of surprise as vital in my life with others, as a way of bringing something new and fresh into my world. Here I will concentrate on one dimension of my childhood, that of definiteness, caliber, determination to be, how it relates to creativity, and its affect on my current thinking and feeling. I plan to invite you along the way to join me in a series of activities as a way of experiencing the processes of creating, willing, and being.

The power to create life is a human capacity that exists in every person. It can never be totally destroyed, for in principle the decision to remain alive and to be assertive is within the individual's scope at all times. The presence of the self, the valuing of my own being, the awareness of who I am and what I believe, ensures an awakening, a clear sense of my own feeling and thinking and an implicit faith in my own experience to guide me and move me forward in my growth.

The valuing of myself is precisely the source of my power, the unique strength that no one can take away—for in the ultimate moments my communion with myself affirms me and enables me to continue to be a particular person who stands out from all others.

Our songs come from the power of our being, the source of unique potential and strength that exists within each of us. When we speak to our powers, when we affirm them, they know we are telling them something. There is an awakening, a response, a return of life. When the sources of life within hear our real voices, they want to listen. If you don't sing your own songs, if you don't play your own music, and speak your own words, if you don't live your own silences, then the powers within you will not know where to find you. They will not know how to work for you.

As a child it was these powers of myself that I listened to, that I talked with, that gave me strength to meet opposition and remain on my own firm ground. I had a way of holding on to what I believed in, valued and wanted. My determination to persist enabled me to continue to be.

Somewhere along the way, I discovered Otto Rank who gave me a great deal to think about in his involvement with the meaning of the will. It was only after repeated resistance that Rank finally recognized the will as a great psychic power. He stated:

> . . . the problem soon presented itself to me as a universal one, going far beyond the critique of psychoanalysis. Why must will be denied if it actually plays so great a role in reality, or to formulate it in anticipation, why is the will valued as bad, evil, reprehensible, unwelcome, when it is the power which consciously and positively, yes even creatively, forms both the self and the environment? Thus the neurotic character represents not illness but a developmental phase of the individuality problem, a personality denying its own will, not accepting itself as an individual.(1)

The power of the will flourishes when we accept and value it. We create life by recognizing and affirming our own selves, for it is we who shape and form ourselves into particular beings in the world. When we respond to the powers within, we move toward new life.

The choosing of my path is an act of will, similar to that performed by the helmsman of a ship, knowing what my ship's course should be and maintaining it, moving forward regardless of the drifts caused by the wind and the currents that would push me off my path. Assagioli has pointed out that staying alive as a self requires willful determination, control, persistence, and initiative.

Consider the turning points or periods of transition in your childhood that depended upon an act of will. Take a few minutes to recall the issue that was the catalyst. Then create a story, scene, or dialogue in which you relate this moment of discovering the power of your own self. Be sure to depict the feelings, the mood, and the impact of this experience. Include in your expression the visual and auditory, and the sense of touch to convey the texture and tone of the experience. When you have created an expression of willful determination from your childhood, find someone important in your life with whom to share this experience.

Martin Buber once stated that every person is an audacity of life, undetermined and unfixed, and therefore requiring confirmation from others. At a pinch one can do without the support of others but one cannot live without affirming one's own self, for supporting one's own self is incontestably more crucial.(3)

Whatever the perceptions of the outside world, we must remain true to our own perceptions and continue to respond to life in accordance with our own selves, however peculiar or idiosyncratic these feelings or views may be. When we stand by ourselves, we learn to listen to our own voices. We experience a feedback effect in feeling our own capability, mastery, trust, and self-esteem returning to us. We continue to be creative by recognizing and affirming the sources of life within ourselves.

I have my way of speaking, but there are always those who want to change me in order to accommodate them. I have learned through my own self-dialogues, through my own self-confirmation, to stand by my own self. I have persisted on my course though others have sometimes tried to push me their way. Quietly, but with determination, I continue to be my own guide; sometimes I find myself traveling alone.

Recently I was severely criticized for not changing my ideas and phrasings to make them more cognitive and "professional" and less filled with feelings and personal references. I was being challenged with questions, with critical faces, belittling asides, and other forms of attack. I responded gently but emphatically that I respected my own language patterns and valued my own personal convictions and feelings. I found myself saying that when I am the speaker it is my responsibility to create from my own self, to let my images, thoughts, and feelings flow. What is at stake is my right to create freely without having to explain, analyze or justify. The words that grow out of my experiences must follow their own course, must be true to the images, metaphors, and symbols that flow from my life. I must be free to continue to fly even when others remain grounded. I must move at my own pace; if it is slow then let it be, and if quick then I shall move swiftly ahead and not look back.

Fortunately I am able to speak for myself. When people hassle me with whisperings and ugly gestures I have a choice—to battle with them or to go on with what I am creating. In the midst of this struggle, I have paused to consider this quotation from Nietzsche.

"They do not understand me: I am not the mouth for these ears.

Perhaps I have lived too long in the mountains, listened too much to the trees and the streams. . . . Unmoved is my soul and bright as the mountains in the morning. . . . And now they look at me and laugh. . . . There is ice in their laughter. . . ."(4)

We all know what happens in classrooms when power is denied children, when it is in the sole control of the teacher. Studies have shown that almost all of the sanctioned conversations that occur in a classroom go from the teacher to the child and back to the teacher again and that almost the only authority, the only source of direction, the source of all answers is the teacher. It doesn't just happen that teachers hold all the power for themselves. They often believe it is essential, that it is necessary to break children, to force them to submit to their authority.

D. H. Lawrence in one of his novels expressed his belief that between teachers and children there will always exist a set of separate wills, each straining to exert its authority. Children will never naturally acquiesce to sitting in a class and submitting to knowledge. They must be forced to do so by a stronger and wiser will, even though they continually strive to revolt. Thus, the first great effort of every teacher is to bring the will of children into accordance with the teacher's own will. This the teacher can do only by applying a system of laws aimed at regulating children's behavior and pressuring them into learning.(5)

This kind of domination is achieved at the expense of freedom, by undermining the integrity and health of the individual. Being free to express oneself and the actual expressions of one's being is an act of will, a sign that the will of the person is still intact. Otto Rank said it some forty-five years ago: ". . . When the patient appears he has already gone through a will conflict usually of quite long duration, which we designate as neurosis."(6)

The whole neurotic conflict is at botton a will conflict. On this conflict, the inability to submit and the inability to put over one's own will positively, the sickness is maintained.

Often the way in which we break a child's will and thus initiate the neurotic process is through the denial of rights, through the use of mental pressures, or through brutality and physical force.

Consider a time in your childhood or currently when you submitted to the will of another person. Return to that relationship with the determination to replay the scene, to stand by your own self. When you have recreated the issue and your determination to change it, select a person with whom to share the experience. Elaborate on your intentions to act in accordance with your own wishes. Keep in mind what the steps are; declare your determination, expand on it, state clearly and boldly your plan of action and stay with it until you feel the full impact and satisfaction of your own will.

In his book, *The End of Tyranny*, Thomas Hanna presents the frightening spectre of the humanoid, the individual almost totally incapable of willing and of acting on intentions, disabled first by parental rearing and later crushed by teachers. The humanoid becomes the authoritarian in society, plagued by an obsession for obedience; always taking cues from the outside; fearful of loss of control, loss of status, loss of security; continually ill at ease in the presence of spontaneity and life, and forever dependent on the support of the group or the team. To quote from Hanna:

> Because humanoids are the fodder of totalitarianism, tyrannical social regimes always attend to the supply of

humanoids. All aspects of public education and public information are controlled by authoritarians so as to guarantee a continuing supply of humanoid fodder. There is no basic distinction between the authoritarian philosophy of education and the techniques of raising livestock; both procedures breed and train living beings for a purpose. And that purpose is defined by the needs of the group that does the breeding and training. (7)

I once observed an incident about a mile from Ypsilanti State Hospital in Michigan. A "patient" was dancing freely down a narrow dirt road. I was so entranced by the glorious movements I paused to watch by the side of the road. All at once, the "patient" became a prey pursued by a number of white-coated men. He ran wildly with all the energy and force of his body, only to be blocked at the end of the road by a hospital ambulance. He was caught and wrestled to the ground. He strained with everything in him until the blood vessels in his neck stood out, stretched and thickened. Finally five men pinned him, tied him up, and tossed him into the back end of the ambulance.

Though Dale and the dancing man were crushed, though they were ultimately controlled by force and violence, still something of great value had happened: Each had found the means to assertiveness, each had valued and affirmed a way of being within, that capacity, that source of life had not been completely broken or destroyed. The will to live was still intact, powerful and strong in the free spaces, in the sunlight, if only for a while. Because each fought with all the powers of the self, that source of inner life had been exercised! Such persons never fully submit to those who would deny growth. They continue to fight with remarkable persistence and determination and with striking individuality.

The gradual eroding of self-assertiveness and self-determination is at the core of human misery and conflict. Our task is not to take over the other person's will, even when the person seeking help requests or demands that we do; our quest is to relate in such a way that the will of the other person is strengthened.

I see the challenge of wills as an essential dimension of any process involving growth in relations, particularly in the American culture where at every turn others are controlling, manipulating, and making decisions. It takes vigilance and constant practice to be able to meet the other person with all the force of one's being and remain intact, to take the buffeting that is inevitable and maintain one's own stronghold of self-direction. Yet this is precisely what is required if a child is to continue to grow as a healthy person. Whatever limits are needed, they must never throttle the will of the child or reduce the child's self-esteem.

When the will is intact, when the self is creative, there are times when the person leaps to an entirely new path, risking, experimenting, moving from inner senses that cannot be known fully. Something undisclosed, unrevealed, perhaps only barely sensed, moves the person to risk and to be daring; as in a trance, life becomes a new creation. Denial of will, failure to respond to these inner glimmerings, holds the person in check and blocks the leaps to new life. The individual accepts the chains, is held by the invisible ties of other persons, and eventually gets into knots that won't let go.

The first challenge of life is the declaration of "I am" and "I will." This leads to becoming a person and to realizing what it means to be human. Part of the process involves deliberation, especially when the expression of the will is not immediate or spontaneous. Then the person struggles, often by experimental dialogue or by rehearsal in imagination and fantasy, testing one alternative and then another, rehearsing again and again to get ready for action. It is essential that the will be expressed, for direct action is needed if the will is to remain strong.

When the will is blocked a counter will or negative will is created or rather the will operates in negative directions. The movement is not toward something positively fulfilling, but rather it is a force against something or someone, sheer opposition or negativism. Generally this happens when a person is rejected; for example, when the child's wishes are cut off and the self of the child is blocked.

There is a way to meet a child when we are in opposition to him or her. One effective approach is to establish limits, real limits, set in a way that does not violate the will of the child. For example, I do not permit a child to club me over the head or throw dangerous objects at me, though a child may strongly want to. I accept his or her desire and may even encourage the expression of feelings against me. I also suggest alternatives, kicking or punching pillows, tearing up paper, coloring or painting angrily, pounding clay, dancing with fury, letting the rage come through. I recognize the child's anger and the child's rights. I encourage the expression of feelings, the engagement of me in violent dialogue, and movement against me. Throughout the process I recognize and affirm the child's will, the child's powers to decide and to choose, to approach me in direct actions or to find alternatives.

The limit is one aspect of an alive experience, the aspect which identifies, characterizes, and distinguishes the dimensions of a relationship. It refers to a unique form and the possibility for life, rather than merely to a limitation.

Because a significant relationship always involves growth, as new experiences occur, patterns emerge that require that limits be established. When limits grow out of a unique reality, they represent not limitations, but a positive presence that makes a particular relationship distinct from every other relationship.

A relationship can only be what it emerges into in experience. A starfish cannot be a starfish without the particular limited form which identifies it as a starfish. It can develop as a starfish and use its capacities only within its own defined structure. Thus real limits provide the boundary or structure in which growth can occur.(8)

When I set a limit it is an aspect of my being, an expression of who I am at a particular moment in time. It is my limit, a boundary of me. When the child accepts the limit a bond is formed between us. The limit is then a structure or boundary of our relationship. It is a reality held in a relationship, not an isolated expression of the individual personalities. The child confirms me, and together we accept a structure through which our relationship can develop.

When the child rejects or breaks the limit it is no longer a reality of a relationship. It is a boundary held by me alone. It no longer has an alive meaning in our relationship. No bond is formed. No structure exists. I literally do not know who I am in *this* relationship. I can withdraw, end the contact, and refuse to participate in an unknown process. Or I can perceive the conflict as an opportunity to face the child freshly and participate in a new dimension of experience.

When I decide to terminate the meeting because a limit has been broken, I will not discover what it means to live with a child who refuses to be denied. I will not know what it is to enter fully as a human being into an emotional dispute or controversy with a child and to see it through to some positive solution.

The expression of anger is an important part of willful communication. Learning to express anger directly is part of the journey in developing a strong and positive will. We may stop the child from carrying out destructive behavior, but we encourage expression of feelings to heighten strong, positive signs of life, "I won't permit you to hit me or throw things at me or break things, but I know you are angry with me and you have every right to be. Tell me how you feel about me. Let me have it with your words."

This approach stops destructive behavior, but it respects the right of children to be angry and encourages children to trust the experience of their own senses, to remain determined, and to feel a sense of mastery. It gives grown-ups an opportunity to listen to children's feelings in a moment of crisis or dispute and to affirm the child as a person of power. Creating feelings of anger is a way of responding to inner sources, a way of being open and direct in relations with others, while maintaining one's own authority and strength.

Only to the extent that we remain with a child through the angry outburst do we reach a healthy solution that strengthens our relationship and recognizes the absolute right of each of us to own our perceptions and feelings. In this way we keep lines of communication open. We permit new awarenesses to emerge that will contribute to the child's sense of power while in no way diminishing our own.

Angry expression is a natural response to frustration, rejection, denial, and strong difference. It is an integral part of being human, to be angry and to show it. It is a way of keeping alive a feeling of caliber and guts, a vibrancy and zest for life.

We should become much more worried when children become complacent, weak and placid, when they readily turn over their fate to other children or adults, when the vital signs of impulse, energy, and spontaneity are dormant, when the will is so diminished that children fail to respond in a situation where anger and self-affirmation are valid protectors of the will. We should be much more concerned when a child's anger is cold and quiet and methodical and devious. Anger not characterized by heated feelings and violent outbursts is often insidious and subtly destructive or manipulating.

In everyday experiences, I see many children expressing both the heated and the methodical type of anger; most often I notice that adults attempt to control explosive anger while they ignore indirect expressions. In my work as a child therapist, I often see children whose backgrounds and conflicts in the family tell me they are filled with rage, but in our initial meetings they express almost no feelings at all. The devious or manipulating behaviors are passive forms of anger but no facial or bodily expressions accompany their actions.

When I meet a child who exhibits anger in a calculating, methodical way, I encourage the child to express his or her feelings directly, even when it means that I will be the target for physical attack. For example, after many play therapy sessions with Donna, one day her feelings reached a peak. She could no longer reject me in a cold and methodical way as she had been doing from our very first meeting. In great frustration she lost control and angrily shot me with a rubber dart gun. I did not stop her. She shot me again and again. I accepted Donna's anger, and her way of expressing it because it was the first open, direct flow of feelings she had expressed in my presence. My intention was to capitalize on the opportunity to encourage

Donna to express her feelings in such a way that she could recognize them as her own, be free of their relentless hold on her, and become more open and direct in her encounters with me and with other children and adults. As paradoxical as it may seem, when Donna had the opportunity to express angry feelings in a direct and open manner, the intensity of her anger and the need to continue expressing it lessened. She declared herself against me, at first by shooting me, but in the process she regained control of her own will. Later, she intensely verbalized her feelings of anger when we were at odds. She was able to express her anger in clear and strong terms without physical attack.

When the original outburst of anger is sharply condemned, and the child is made to feel small and mean and guilty, then the fixed attitude of deception becomes a focal point in the child's world. Gradually the child becomes insensitive and responds without feeling in the presence of pain and injustice. So it is imperative to permit children the freedom to be angry and to express their feelings, to affirm this right again and again. Later in life when a situation calls for forthright, independent action and valid indignation, feelings of anger and the ability to express them will have a seasoned and powerful impact. Standing alone and being in opposition, the will comes through with appropriate intelligence and effective action.

Consider now a relationship you are involved in currently or one that you have been involved in recently with a child where there has been a clash of wills and strong opposition. Return to that relationship. Imagine a new type of dialogue and action between you and the child, where you respect the child's stubbornness or willfulness, yet you set a limit. Write a poem or story or dialogue in which a creative confrontation with the child is portrayed, in which there is movement to a positive resolution. Share this with someone you value as a way of opening a discussion of creative conflict where the wills of both persons remain intact and are affirmed and strengthened.

One of my most exciting hours in some time occurred recently with Jim, a late teen-ager, whom I'd first seen in therapy as a five-year-old, diagnosed as a mentally retarded child. I'd maintained a friendship with him over the years. On this day, he had come to enlist my support in a plan that would totally emancipate him from his parents. On the basis of my knowledge of him and his struggle with drugs and alcohol, I opposed the plan and offered a counterproposal, which he immediately rejected. For the remainder of the hour we grappled in opposition. It did not matter who would win or lose, who would be victorious or defeated. What mattered was that each of us fully engaged the other, fully exercised our wills, and in the process each of us drew from the other all that we had to offer. We both sharpened our awarenesses, came up with new ideas, and continued to see different alternatives for action. Thus we were challenged to use all our powers as partners in opposition. Fortunately, because over the years I had affirmed Jim's will at every opportunity, I was now benefiting by the fervor, openness, directness, no-holds-barred way in which he came forth to meet me. As he left, he shouted "I've trusted you ever since I was knee high to a grasshopper. And whatever you finally recommend, I'll seriously consider." I liked that, for he was saying that though he respected my judgment he was clearly in charge of his life.

Let's try two more activities in exercising the will. First, get into a relaxed position and close your eyes. Now consider a person in your current life or in the past who stopped you from doing something you strongly wanted to do, stopped you from expressing your will. Select a situation where you actually gave in, surrendered, didn't do the thing you wanted to do. Now imagine yourself, or perhaps this actually happened, becoming very upset with yourself that you choked off your own will and allowed the other person to have that power over you. Imagine yourself going back to that person and this time declaring yourself, asserting strongly that you will do this thing and he or she won't stop you. Be determined, definite, clear, and strong about your plan and the execution of it. Take a few minutes to rehearse the situation. Now contact a friend and share your plan of action. Use your voice, pound, move around—in every way let your friend know your intention. In clear terms express your determination and assert your will.

This time take a few minutes to recapture a situation where you did something that you really didn't want to do, where you surrendered to the other person's wish or will. Perhaps currently there's someone in your life who is determined to get you to do something that you don't want to do. Create a scene in your fantasy and rehearse what you will do or say to that person. When you feel the power rising go face the person who is demanding that you act against your will. Let that person know without reservation that you have absolutely no intention of doing that thing, that everything in you is against it. Feel what it is like to be in charge of your own self, to declare your own fate.

It is essential from the beginning and continuing through life that we develop a strong sense of self, a definite sense of "I am" and of "I will." Again and again in play, in work, in self-exploration, and in communication with others we must be assertive if we are to grow firm, strong, definite. The declaration of the self is a way of saying "Yes" and "No." In both cases we are exercising our will and gaining practice in being persons, in realizing what it means to be unique human beings, persons who say clearly, strongly, independently "I will" and "I won't." The exercising of the will leads to a genuine identity. We know who we are and others clearly recognize us. Once given up, the will is lost, or buried, and as the will is weakened the being or self of the person is also weakened. This is like giving up one's soul. When we surrender our soul to others or to things, we face a life-long struggle to recover and restore it. It is like the loss of the sun for a long, long time, when there is only darkness and a life without vibrancy and color. Everything is dimmed or at best life brightens only when someone else lights the candle, only when someone else is around to lead us, to make our decisions for us, and to tell us how to act and how to be.

REFERENCES

1. RANK, OTTO. *Will Therapy and Truth and Reality.* Tr. by Jessie Taft. New York: Alfred A. Knopf, 1950. p. 221.
2. ASSAGIOLI, ROBERTO. *The Act of Will.* Baltimore: Penguin Books, Inc., p. 19.
3. BUBER, MARTIN. *Between Man and Man.* Tr. by Ronald Gregor Smith. London: K. Paul, 1947.
4. NIETZSCHE, FRIEDRICH. *Thus Spake Zarathustra.* Baltimore: Penguin Books, 1961, p. 47.
5. LAWRENCE, D. H. *The Rainbow.* New York: The Viking Press, 1961, p. 383.

6. RANK, OTTO. *Ibid.*, p. 16.

7. HANNA, THOMAS. *The End of Tyranny.* San Francisco: Freeperson Press, 1975, pp. 49-50.

8. MOUSTAKAS, CLARK. *Psychotherapy With Children.* New York: Harper & Row, 1959.

Freedom
To Learn
And To Be

When I consider turning points that have stood out in the development of my values, I inevitably return to my life in public schools where for many years I responded mechanically to the dictates of teachers, where I went through the motions of learning, without the slightest involvement or presence as a self. From my first school days when teachers attempted to mold my Greek speech into standard English, I knew from the inside that something was radically wrong, that authoritarian demands were violating my right to learn with dignity, in a unified way, with my right to make choices and to maintain the uniqueness and distinctiveness of my own self. What held me to the fixed routines was my belief that that was the way school life was supposed to be, that being in prison as a student was the natural state of affairs, and that the laws of society required it. I did not realize that learning need not be sterile, closed, and impeding of real growth. My way of handling the issue was to meet the external requirements mechanically, with dispatch, and then to go quickly underground, where there was excitement and energy, to fashion my own thinking, feeling, and imagining. In spite of the constant push for conformity, I found indirect ways of asserting myself, of developing my autonomy, and of trusting my own senses to guide me in the learning process. In one way or another I left distinctive marks of my self in everything I undertook but they were evident only to me.

When finally the revelation came that laws of learning or of society did not require that freedom and individuality be squelched, then and there I declared my independence as a learner and vowed that I would never again pursue knowledge on the basis of others' preferences, dictates, or standards. In that moment I declared my allegiance to learning based on inspiration, on self-interest, and on individual goals. Whatever was essential in learning and growing I would master in my own way, with my own resources for observing, testing, and assimilating. That day of awakening to what real learning is and means, of realizing in a conscious and deliberate sense what it means to be alive as a learner and to create new life, represents a critical turning point. My whole world changed as I selected the books and other published resources that I wanted to read, pursued interests that moved and excited me, and developed skills that made sense to me. In general I brought my underground thrusts out into the light of day.

My belief in the crucial significance of freedom in learn-

ing, in the right of the person to be, and in the value of
choice and interest in the process of becoming, continue to
be central in all of my involvements in the learning process.

As I write this, I am looking into late fall in Michigan,
into a forest of trees—each in a different place in the
movement toward winter. I notice leaves blowing to the
ground, and view a panorama of fading colors. I am
amazed at the variation, the striking individuality, the u-
niqueness of the process. I am impressed with the freedom
of movement, trees rooted yet swaying beautifully with the
wind. An array of sizes and shapes and patterns fill a por-
tion of the sky, trees standing alone yet blending together.
Wherever I look I discover something new, something in-
triguing. Here before me is the consequence of freedom,
individuality, and uniqueness in nature. Human beings
start life with these same values. But then, very soon, every
effort is made to rob them of this natural heritage. When
people are aware of what is happening they learn quickly
that they must be vigilant, that they must battle constantly
to maintain their freedom, individuality, and uniqueness.

I permit these distressing thoughts to fade and pause
once more to experience the beauty of natural life before
me. I feel an excitement in being alive right now in the
midst of this distinctive fall splendor. I am experiencing
the thrilling sensations of a new morning, and for a while a
totally peaceful life. As I consider the wonders of nature,
all at once other strong images emerge, of long ago during
my very first seminar with teachers, administrators, and
counselors, in my beginning efforts to bring human values
into the learning process, into the public school classroom.

I had gathered with twenty people from a metropolitan
Detroit school system to offer a course entitled "Freedom

in Learning." Advance word that I was bringing a pre-scription for rebellion into the schools had been spread, for only an hour after we began the Superintendent of Schools entered furiously into our meeting and demanded to know what I intended to do in *his* schools. I suggested that he listen for a while. I made but two statements when he interrupted again. I had stated that: "Without freedom there can be no real learning" and "Being free is a natural human state that can either be enhanced toward individu-ality and creativity or thwarted in favor of standardization and conformity." He screamed that freedom in the class-room always led to chaos. Fortunately, others in the group intervened and spoke of their own experiments with freedom and the creative variations that were emerg-ing. They pointed out that often freedom began with chaos, but that from the chaos an entirely new way of learning and relating was emerging, that they were coming to know children as individuals and were discovering ways to facilitate the learning process. I entered the discussion with a quote from Nietzsche, "I tell you one must have chaos in one, to give birth to a dancing star. Alas! The time is coming when man will give birth to no more stars."(1) The mere mention of Nietzsche threw the superintendent into a panic. He shouted something like: "I don't want any damned chaos or dancing stars in my schools." With that outburst, he left us to pursue our study of human values in learning. Within a week the superintendent threatened to fire me, but as I was employed by Wayne State University in Detroit, that was not an option for him. Angrily, he came to my seminars the next several meetings but stayed only a short time. At the end of the semester, he termi-nated his contract with Wayne. At the end of the school year, the Board of Education terminated their contract with him. I returned for the next three years to the same school system, working with a new group each year, until a nucleus was formed for making freedom and individuality central concerns in the learning process in that school system. The story of my encounters with a number of school systems and the inclusion of principles and practices from therapy into classroom communication and relationships is told in detail in my books, *Teaching As Learning* and *The Authentic Teacher*.(2,3)

Freedom is still a central value in my involvement with schools. It is still the place I begin. Once freedom is denied, learners begin to erect defenses and either conform or fight. Sometimes the battles are indirect and devious; sometimes, though it is a child against grown-ups, the battle is waged out in the open. Whether the individual conforms or fights, energies are being used to defend a position and learning is deterred and blocked.

Nowhere is the fight for freedom more pronounced than in the schools. Even if children have won out over the repressive influences of family and society; even if they have been loved as free spirits and their uniqueness has been enhanced rather than tampered with; the big challenge comes in the schools, where powerful tactics are used, including one's own peers, to squelch and defeat the child who protests, the one who is different, the person who stands by his own style, preferences, interests, and beliefs.

At the very heart of freedom is the self of the person. In every violation of freedom the integrity of the individual is denied. Being free to express oneself, the actual expressions of one's being, is an act of self-affirmation, a sign of healthy life.

Closely related to freedom and individuality is the value

of authenticity. A person is either present in a learning process or is role playing and engaging in stereotyped modes of behaving. Nobody is more aware of this than the person who suddenly realizes that the activities and actions of everyday living have no real meaning when they are based on others' preferences, expectations, and standards.

In dealing with authenticity in the classroom, I distinguish between motivation and inspiration. Motivation is an external system of known limits, with specific purposes and goals, on a closed path. As generally used in schools, motivation comes from the persons in charge. They aim to influence learners to engage in projects that fulfill the goals of the establishment. Tensions are created by those in authority, usually through a program of incentives, rewards and consequences, and these tensions are then resolved through the fulfillment of assignments and through evaluation and grades. The most effective way follows a straight line with competition often used as the motivating force that distinguishes the superior student from those who are mediocre or inferior. Here is an example from an elementary school classroom:

> It is boys versus girls. . . . A small boy comes forward for 7+2 and guesses at 8. The boys groan; the girls cheer; the teacher looks pained. The "motivation" is high. There is good attention and "involvement." It's a good lesson—by normal standards. It seems that the girls frequently win. The chagrined boy returns to his seat and while his efficient teacher continues through *her lesson*, which she imagines is arithmetic, the real lesson is demonstrated in front of me as the little boy punches the little girl next to him as hard as he can, saying, "I hate you, I hate you, I hate you."(4)

In another illustration, Jules Henry speaks of Boris, a

fifth grader, at the board attempting to reduce a fraction to its lowest terms. He is performing for the teacher and the class, and he is being judged. While he works, he is being assigned a status and a role that he will carry with him for the rest of his school life and probably afterwards in the world of work. On this day, he is having trouble reducing a fraction; the teacher suggests that he "think." His classmates wave their hands up and down, all frantic to correct Boris. Finally, the teacher gives up with Boris and calls on Peggy, who always knows the right answers. Jules Henry continues:

> Thus Boris' failure has made it possible for Peggy to succeed; his depression is the price of her exhilaration, his misery the occasion of her rejoicing. This is the standard condition of the American elementary school. . . . Peggy's action seems natural to us; and so it is. How else could you run our world? And since all but the brightest children have the constant experience that others succeed at their expense, they cannot but develop an inherent tendency to hate—to hate the success of others, to hate others who are successful, and to be determined to prevent it. Along with this, naturally, goes the hope that others will fail. . . . Looked at from Boris' point of view, the nightmare at the blackboard was, perhaps, a lesson in controlling himself so that he would not fly shrieking from the room under the enormous public pressure.(5)

In the competitive standard, time is always a factor, the pressures of time, the urgency to finish fast because faster is always better. Everything is time-oriented, scheduled and valued in time. In the competitive process, there are always labels to motivate and push learners, labels to fix individuals, forms of prophesying and forecasting that put children in molds and deprive them of authentic feelings and choices, names that are substitutes for real expressions of real persons. When we call a person dumb or stupid or lazy we are ingraining that characteristic into the person, just as directly as when we put a bump there. Labels are missiles that undermine and restrict and lead people astray. They are really substitutes for reality, but they sometimes become so entrenched that many people are able to understand only when something is defined, measured, and labeled, as in this poem of D. H. Lawrence:

> What is he?
> —A man, of course.
> Yes, but what does he do?
> —He lives and is a man.
> Oh quite! but he must work. He must have a job of some
>   sort.
> —Why?
> Because obviously he's not of the leisured classes.
> —I don't know. He has lots of leisure. And he makes quite
>   beautiful chairs.—
> There you are then! He's a cabinet maker.
> —No no!
> Anyhow a carpenter and joiner.
> —Not at all.
> But you said so.
> —What did I say?
> That he made chairs, and was a joiner and carpenter.
> —I said he made chairs, but I did not say he was a
>   carpenter.
> All right then, he's just an amateur.
> —Perhaps! Would you say a thrush was a professional
>   flautist, or just an amateur?
> I'd say it was just a bird.
> —And I say he is just a man.
> All right! You always did quibble.(6)

The competition game is not the only one that contributes to alienation and the denial of authenticity. Other techniques include the use of punishment, group pressures, the everyday facades, the fake communications, the use of invisible enemies and authorities to justify rules and procedures, and all the other forms of betrayal and hypocrisy that are direct roads to dehumanizing and alienating children from themselves and others.

In contrast to motivation, inspiration comes from inner sources of awareness and feeling and energy. The path of inspiration moves outward to touch new life; the road is unknown and open-ended. Rarely does such a path follow a straight line but moves in nonlinear directions and bypaths.

Being inspired, learners enter timelessly, pursuing a question, a problem, an area of interest, completely centered and absorbed.

When cooperation is central in learning, children grow from each other; they learn to share abilities and resources and delight in the positive changes they are able to facilitate in each other. Here's an example from a classroom where cooperation is valued. With a great deal of excitement and pride, Mrs. Henderson shared the following:

> Danny is one of the fastest readers in the class but he often does not comprehend what he reads. Willie is great in comprehension but he reads ever so haltingly. So I decided to put the two boys together, suggesting to Danny that he help Willie read faster and to Willie that he help Danny understand what he reads. After a month this team work began to pay off. I noticed a drastic change with Danny vastly improved in comprehension and Willie reading at a more flowing rate.

In a human climate of learning, as Campbell unequivocally states,

... children change in a short time from mistrustful, hating, suspicious, and terribly destructive children into real children who begin to trust again, help one another, smile and laugh in school and who do not want to leave for recess, lunch, or even home. They look forward to every day. It is no miracle; it requires time, but entails nothing much more than minimizing and finally removing the sorting, ranking, and labeling role of schools. It involves stopping the failure. It means establishing a classroom where competition is not used as a motivation for learning. Kids in our society may always engage in some competition, but it is not the teacher's job to promote it, for it has nothing to do with education.(7)

Abraham Maslow has emphasized that effective education in music, art, dancing, and rhythm is far closer to real learning and to life than the usual "core curriculum." If education doesn't help a person know and become who he or she is, it is useless. Maslow points out, "Education is learning to grow, learning what to grow toward, learning what is good and bad, learning what is desirable and undesirable, learning what to choose and what not to choose." The arts, and especially music, dancing and rhythms, art, and literature, are close to our psychological and biological core. Rather than treat these courses as luxuries, they must become basic experiences in education. Such experiences, Maslow says, beginning with two-, three-, and four-year-old children, "could very well serve as the model, the means by which perhaps we could rescue the rest of the school curriculum from the valueless, meaningless programs into which it has fallen."(8)

My current involvement in schools has not been in open classrooms as such or in any specific structure, but rather *I have focused on the human classroom, recognizing and affirming those values and guiding principles that awaken the individual to new life within and without and that support authentic interaction with the self and others.* The human atmosphere encourages every child to experiment, explore, and relate through play media and academic resources.

We start with life—with whatever is life-enhancing. Living means growing! What is dead has ceased to grow. Growth occurs in a real way only when the individual wills it. Thus to learn, to change, or to grow we awaken the life that is within. We recognize our own power to initiate learning and value our own path, which is the real path to growth.

When grown-ups impose their standards of what is desirable, when they tell children what to do, they bypass the only genuine source of learning, the wellsprings of life that are within each person.

Here are two examples of adults pushing children to perceive their way:

In the first, a father is quizzing his young son while waiting for breakfast to be served.

> What state do you live in?
>   Michigan
> What's the largest city in Michigan?
>   Detroit
> What state is due south of Michigan?
>   I don't know
> I've drilled you and drilled you and
>   you still don't know
> You always put your words
>   into my mouth

The second example comes from *Love*, Leo Bascuglia's book:

"Boys and girls, today we are going to draw a tree." She goes to the board, and she draws her tree which is a great big green ball with a little brown base. Remember those lollipop trees? I never saw a tree that looked like that in my life, but she puts it up there, and she says, "All right boys and girls, draw." Everybody gets busy and draws.

If you have any sense, even at that early age, you realize that what she really wanted was for you to draw *her* tree, because the closer you got to her tree, the better your grade. If you already realized this in grade one, then you handed in a little lollipop, and she said, "Oh, that's divine." But here's Junior who really knows a tree as this little woman has never seen a tree in her life. He's climbed a tree, he's hugged a tree, he's fallen out of a tree, he's listened to the breeze blow through the branches. He really knows a tree, and he knows a tree isn't a lollipop. So he takes purple and yellow and orange and green and magenta crayons and he draws this beautiful freaky thing and hands it in. She takes one look and shrieks, "brain damaged!"(9)

In order to grow, like all living beings, children must have freedom—freedom to discover, to be aware, to move toward learning that is exciting and satisfying, learning that contributes to self-esteem. When rules and regulations and standards take the place of freedom, children move quickly from life that is within waiting to grow, to leaning and depending on others, and eventually to stagnation and death. They begin to feel helpless and small, unable to choose and to decide. They constantly want to be told what to do, what is right or wrong, even when no adults are around. I have seen many children defeated by the power and authority of grown-ups, disabled in their own senses, in their own judgment and ability to know and to act. In play therapy, from the start children have the freedom to decide what they want to do. They often remain frozen in the center of the room unable to move or decide. Even when they insist, I won't tell them what to do. It is up to them to become aware of desires and preferences, to make choices and to create a life of their own. Albert Einstein, speaking out of his own experience in educational institutions, registers this frightening observation: "It is in fact nothing short of a miracle that the modern methods of instruction have not yet entirely strangled the holy curiosity of inquiry; for this delicate little plant, aside from stimulation, stands mainly in need of freedom; without this it goes to wrack and ruin without fail."

Denial of freedom, loss of self-esteem, rejection of the wisdom of personal choices, creates feelings of helplessness and dependency. Many children are unable to be effective when the power person is not around. One of the most common consequences of temporary loss of the person with power is fear. Loss of the presence of the power person also creates feelings of being unloved and feelings of helplessness.

As the usual curriculum ignores the resources and powers of children for self-directed learning, a deliberate effort must now be made to reawaken sources of self-discovery and self-expression. We must first of all recognize the validity of the senses, experience what we see, touch, feel, taste, and smell. We must trust in that which is our own and know that we are on the right path. We must provide for individual differences, recognize the uniqueness of learning, and offer options and alternatives rather than imposing one learning resource, one activity, one task.

In my involvement with young children I encourage them to exercise their senses by creating a wide range of activities. We walk to touch a variety of textures, to smell a wide range of odors and fragrances, to notice colors, shapes, ranges of what there is to see in surrounding neighborhoods and in nature. We listen for the multiplicity of sounds. And we sample a variety of tastes. Each child creates a book of pictures, drawings, paintings, cutouts from magazines, and sometimes words and phrases that emphasize the particularity of learning—the sounds that are pleasant and those which are objectionable; the tastes which are satisfying, those that are unpleasant. We take journeys of many kinds—seeing, noticing, becoming aware; listening, hearing, distinguishing, touching, surfaces, textures, shapes; smelling, sweet, pungent; tasting, sour, sweet, bitter. We take nature trips, neighborhood trips, and others. Children tell their stories, draw murals, use words and pictures, create a book of sense experiences with words, phrases, stories, poems, pictures. With each of the sense avenues I encourage freedom, choice, individuality, creativity, imagination, and self-expression. Through each child's creations a clear picture unfolds of that child's unique path of learning.

To reintroduce these values that return the powers of learning and creation to the learner, we begin with the senses and with feelings and we return to the earliest bases for human communication and growth—art, music, literature, and movement.(10)

I encourage children to go wide open with fingerpainting, drawings, and water colors. In one group I worked with, the teacher, Mrs. Dover, took a long while to give up the reins but eventually she became convinced of the value of giving back the power of learning to the learner. To my surprise one morning she devised an experience in which she integrated art, movement, storytelling, public speaking, and interviewing. She made her own finger paints, selected a Temptations album, spread paper around the floor, and invited the children to close their eyes, relax, and think about a story that would tell of one of their happiest times. She asked them, instead of telling the story, to express it through finger painting. She wanted the visual, the tactile, and the feeling components to be included with the cognitive. While the children painted, she played the record "On Cloud Nine," and within moments they began to move—some amazingly well with their whole bodies, as they painted. Afterwards, the children told their stories into a microphone, and the stories were recorded while Mrs. Dover held up each painting so all could see. After each child, Mrs. Dover conducted an interview to encourage more expression of feelings and to derive a list of activities that would create happiness for that child in the classroom. Photography, games, music, trips, scrapbooks, special foods, and dramatics were high on the list. As the year unfolded, each of these was given a sustained place in the "curriculum."

We are concerned with children's feelings and select children's stories and musical compositions that deal with anger, fear, joy, and loneliness. Each major emotion is given an emphasis. With loneliness, for example, we might use a story like *Crow Boy* or *Evan's Corner* to emphasize the value of solitude or the feelings of rejection and fear connected with loneliness. (11, 12) We might read or tell the story to create an atmosphere or mood. We always begin with the climate that provides the ground out of which the specific experience will emerge. Always we direct ourselves to awareness, then to centering or concentrating and finally to action.

Anger is a feeling that requires special attention from us. We respond to the anger of the child by accepting it. We encourage the expression of anger through punching, kicking, and in many other ways, but we also encourage children to express their feelings of anger in words. Sometimes we read stories that focus on anger and ask children to express their feelings on paper.

Many spontaneous, angry feelings are expressed. When there is conflict among children we stop physical attack, but we encourage children to use words and gestures to express their feelings. Sometimes children express their anger in play, using puppets to portray family scenes of conflict as ways of releasing anger toward brothers, sisters, or friends. We emphasize two things: First, express the anger in ways that will not be self-destructive or destructive to others. Second, understand what precipitates the anger so there is a choice of whether to pursue it or not. We assist children in finding their way back to freedom and their own self-esteem by helping them to confront their feelings of anger.

I would like to suggest an activity for your participation that would be similar to our approach with children. Join a group of three other people, get into a relaxed position, and close your eyes. Recall your most recent experience of anger. Who were you angry at? What did you say or do? What did the other person say or do? Recreate the scene. Now this time express honestly and directly all the feelings you didn't express before. Put everything into your communication of anger. When all the feelings are out, pay attention to what precipitated the anger and make some decision about how you will handle it in the future.

Now share this experience with the other members of your group. Select one of the scenes of anger and dramatize it, putting into the scene all the heated words and actions; pantomime and gestures are encouraged, but no physical contact.

We have discovered that fear is often at the bottom of the inability to decide, to act, to play, to be on one's own, and to create a good life for oneself. In Rosenbaum and McAuliffe's book *What Is Fear?*, the story of Grace's extreme fear is communicated. When she was little, her parents worked and she was left with many baby-sitters. Grace didn't like her sitters very much, and she began to feel lonely. She worried that no one cared about her. She wanted her parents to stay home, but they had to work. Grace really didn't understand. All she knew was that her parents weren't there and that there was nothing she could do about it.

The story continues:

> She'd say, "Don't turn the lights off! There's a big bear under my bed and he'll come out and eat me up if you turn off the lights."
>
> Her parents tried to convince her that there wasn't any bear under her bed. But Grace wouldn't listen. Darkness made her feel so lonely and scared she was sure there actually had to be something dangerous in her room. . . . She began to have nightmares. In her dreams she could see the ground opening up and horrible goblins crawling out. She would try to run but she couldn't get away. The goblins were reaching for her and her legs wouldn't move. . . . Deep down inside, Grace was actually furious with her parents for leaving her every day. But she couldn't admit it. What would they think if they found out that she wanted to scream and throw things at them? Grace believed they would abandon her. She thought she *deserved* to be abandoned because she was so angry.

Eventually, with help, Grace began to talk about her feelings. First to her friends and later to her parents. She discovered that neither her parents nor her friends would abandon her because of what she felt. If she became angry with them, they might get angry back—but they wouldn't stop loving her.

Grace got over her fear of the dark. She learned that she was not alone, and she also learned that she was not helpless. Anger did not turn her into a monster.(13)

What happened to Grace happened because her own power and control were transferred to her parents. Without them she was a nobody. Somewhere along the way in growing up she learned she didn't count, she had no rights, she had no voice in choosing her own destiny. Everything came from them; everything depended on them.

When this persists through the years, the person is terrified to be alone. We then must help children find their way back to freedom, to courage, to creative expression. Play and rehearsals of fears through play materials and drama, sharing and open communication help children face the real situations, help them confront and resolve their fears.

In an encouraging climate children test out their feelings and pursue their interests. There is a growing awareness, an increased focus and concentration, an eventual expression. Sometimes it helps to affirm and expand awareness through imagination and fantasy. In *Put Your Mother on the Ceiling* children are guided through a series of activities in which they exercise imagination with reference to mother, school, weights, body awareness, and other dimensions of their world. Here is an example:

> Let us imagine your school room. / Let us have it empty. / No one in the seats. No one at the teacher's desk. No one at the blackboard. / Look all around the school room and see that there is no one there. Now, you be at the front of the room, teaching all the empty chairs. / Have books and pencils and papers at every place. / Have the pencils writing on the paper. / Have the pages of the books turning. / Have pieces of chalk writing on the

blackboard. / Have the pieces of paper come up the front of the room, to be graded. Have a school room full of children. / You be teaching them. / Have one boy put up his hand and ask to leave the room. / Let him go. / Have the others write a spelling lesson on their papers. / Have them add some numbers. / Send some of them to the blackboard to draw pictures.

What else would you like to do in your imagination school?

Now let's play a game called Heavy:

Let us imagine that you are walking down the street. / Lean down and pick up a penny. / Throw it over your shoulder. / Pick up a baseball. / Throw it over your shoulder. / Pick up a watermelon and throw it over your shoulder. / Hear it break when it hits the street. / Look back and see the seeds scattered all over.

Pick up a suitcase and throw it over your shoulder. / Pick up a horse that is standing there and throw it over your shoulder. / Pick up an automobile and throw it over your shoulder. / Pick up a truck and throw it over your shoulder.

Lean down and try to pick up a toy dog. / Have the dog be too heavy to pick up. / Have two big men trying to pick the dog up, but have it be too heavy. / Have a machine trying to pick the dog up, but have it be too heavy. / You pick up the dog. / Have the dog kiss you.

What would you like to pick up now?(14)

Another approach to creativity and imagination is through the writing of poetry. In *Wishes, Lies, and Dreams*, for example, children are invited to create poems using colors, comparisons, dreams, and wishes.(15) Stephen Joseph has observed that when children are asked to write poetry, they almost always protest at first, but as they begin to find their own ways of putting feelings into words, poetry becomes a valued and natural medium of expression.(16)

Finally, we emphasize communication and relationships, the importance of listening and accepting. The DUSO materials have been helpful, with their songs, stories, messages, puppets, and posters.(17) We often create exercises that facilitate empathy in body communication, nonverbal messages, and effectiveness in relating back what another person is saying. Eventually, we put everything into an active process. Whatever is being learned is expressed through role-playing and dramas, through rhythms and movement, through dancing, stories, painting and drawing, poetry. I will present but one example: Margo responded to the sudden death of her mother by repressing her fear and anger. Through our discussions of hospital experiences, of illness, of disease and death, Margo began to relate her feelings. In the dance-a-story, with pantomime, movement, and dance, she recreated the whole period of her mother's illness, hospitalization, and death. Later she put this story into a mural that included pictures, poetry, and song; thus visual art and body expression were Margo's choices for communication and release. We very much support Nietzsche's conviction:

"You say 'I' and you are proud of this word. But greater than this—although you will not believe in it—is your body and its great intelligence, which does not say 'I' but performs 'I'."(18) By performing "I," Margo let go of the tensions within her, maintained a connection with her mother, and began a new life of her own.

We often work with individuals. In my book *Loneliness and Love*, I presented several examples of special classroom

contacts with the lonely child, and in *Learning To Be Free*
there are numerous instances of responding to the angry
and the joyous child.(19,20) We meet life where it is.
Sometimes only a few minutes are needed to free a child
from the pain and anguish of rejection. Our entire thrust
is to awaken, affirm, recognize; to provide resources and
opportunities for expression and release; to move life
from terror to beauty, from tension to tranquility, from
fear to courage. We move the world of learning and doing
from monotony and death to energy and new life.

Looking back I know now that the discovery of the violence to life in my own early education, my ultimate declaration of independence as a learner, my resolve to remain
free, to nourish privacy and autonomy, to create life from
within, was the beginning of a transformation of self, a
movement from denial to recognition, from rejection to
nourishment, from competition to cooperation, from
being closed to becoming open, from restraint to freedom.
These values have continued to be central in my choice of
paths, in my life in the classroom, in my family, and in the
world.

REFERENCES

1.   NIETZSCHE, FRIEDRICH. *Thus Spake Zarathustra*. Tr. by R. J.
     Hollingdale. Baltimore: Penguin Books, 1961, p. 46.
2.   MOUSTAKAS, CLARK. *Teaching As Learning*. New York: Bal-
     lantine Books, Inc., 1972.
3.   MOUSTAKAS, CLARK. *The Authentic Teacher*. Cambridge,
     Mass.: Howard A. Doyle Publishing Co., 1966.
4.   CAMPBELL, DAVID N. "On Being Number One: Competi-
     tion in Education." *Phi Delta Kappan*, Oct. 1974, p. 143.

5. HENRY, JULES. *Culture Against Man*. New York: Random House, Inc., 1963, p. 296.

6. LAWRENCE, D. H. *The Complete Poems of D. H. Lawrence*. Vol. 1, ed. by Vivian de Sola Pinto and Warren Roberts. New York: The Viking Press, 1964, pp. 452-453.

7. CAMPBELL, DAVID N. *Op. cit.*, p. 145.

8. MASLOW, A. H. *The Farther Reaches of Human Nature*. New York: The Viking Press, 1971, pp. 178-179.

9. BUSCUGLIA, LEO F. *Love*. Thorofare, N.J.: C. B. Slack, 1972, p. 10.

10. MOUSTAKAS, CLARK and CERETA PERRY. *Learning To Be Free*. Englewood Cliffs, N.J.: Prentice-Hall, 1973.

11. YACHIMA, T. *Crow Boy*. New York: Viking, 1955.

12. HILL, ELIZABETH STARR. *Evan's Corner*. New York: Holt, Rinehart and Winston, Inc., 1967.

13. ROSENBAUM, JEAN and LUTIE MCAULIFFE. *What Is Fear?* Englewood Cliffs, N.J.: Prentice-Hall, 1972, p. 11.

14. DEMILLE, RICHARD. *Put Your Mother on the Ceiling*. New York: The Viking Press, 1973, pp. 83–84; pp. 154–156.

15. KOCH, KENNETH. *Wishes, Lies, and Dreams*. New York: Chelsea House Publishers, 1970.

16. JOSEPH, STEPHEN. *The Me Nobody Knows*. New York: Avon Books, 1969, pp. 11–12.

17. DINKMEYER, DON. "DUSO Kit D-1." Circle Pines, Minn.: Amer. Guidance Service, Inc.

18. NIETZSCHE, FRIEDRICH. *Ibid.*, p. 62.

19. MOUSTAKAS, CLARK. *Loneliness and Love*. Englewood Cliffs, N.J.: Prentice-Hall, 1972.

20. MOUSTAKAS, CLARK, and CERETA PERRY. *Learning To Be Free*. Englewood Cliffs, N.J.: Prentice-Hall, 1973.

The Creative
Path Of
Loneliness

The recognition of loneliness as a creative process was a major turning point in my adult life. For the first time I began to see how many of the significant changes in my personal growth and in my relations with others were connected with feelings of loneliness. This awareness and the acceptance of myself as a lonely person enabled me to retreat into regions I had not dared face earlier, movement into wild dreams and fantasies, into strange symbols and images, and into an expanded consciousness that transcended tangible, concrete happenings and encouraged silence and a trancelike presence. When I remained with these processes, I realized the importance of standing by my private perceptions and permitting them to travel in their own way, respecting my intuitions, sensings, and feelings as they related to life. Often these lonely pilgrimages helped me to face issues and to gain the courage to be my own self even when this meant being at odds with others, apart from conventions, and isolated. My valuing of the lonely life enabled me to grow from the center of my being.

In times of loneliness, my way back to life with others required that I stop listening to others, that I cut myself off from others and deliberately go off alone, to a place of isolation. I found it necessary to tune into my own internal states. Sometimes feelings sparked immediately and I became aware of how I had forsaken myself, how I had drifted away from my inner life, and how important it was to come back home to me. Sometimes in my place of isolation I would engage in conversations with myself as a way of putting thoughts and feelings out into the open and clarifying what was happening in my life, what I wanted to do, what was missing, how I wanted to commit my energies. Often there was struggle and pain with the realization that somehow I was not fully living a life of meaning but was avoiding or ignoring inner states and too much involved in social or professional contacts. I needed to return to a sense of privacy and to dialogues with my own self. This kind of awakening was often initiated by feelings of alienation, of being with others yet feeling deeply alone, or by a crisis or disenchantment with life that left me feeling empty, tense, and depressed. In solitude, silent awareness and self-dialogues often quickly restored me to myself and I was filled with new energy and the desire to renew my life with others in real ways. I resolved to stay with one other person or with a group as long as I felt alive as a person, as long as I could maintain my individuality while communicating with others in a real way.

There were times in my loneliness when silence and

conversations with myself were not enough for me to grow into a new life, to remove the anxiety of feeling separate and apart and lonely. My sense of loneliness at such times required something more boldly expressive, something more definite, more assertive. When the path finally began to emerge, I realized that only some creative process, some total expression, would satisfy. Sometimes sounds would come from my body—at first, chaotic, weird, pronounced, uncontrolled. Staying with these sounds, I began to chant sometimes in a discordant and unbalanced way but ultimately the chanting moved to rhythms. Finally a pattern formed. I had found my way into a poem or a song and with it came new hope; the sense of dread and despair was over. I was no longer fighting my loneliness. I was no longer avoiding or denying it. I was relating to it, finding a way to use the energy of loneliness in creative pursuits. I welcomed my loneliness, greeted it warmly, accepted it as part of me. I was on good terms with it. Being lonely was not something dreadful but simply a part of my life.

I discovered that living with loneliness required patience, a willingness to wait, to experience my boredom, or emptiness, or feeling separate and apart, to recognize my low energy, simply to notice these feelings but not be overwhelmed by them or in any way disown them, notice that they were part of me and not sink into abject despair or run away from such feelings. Ultimately there was a turning point; my waiting, my patience, my acceptance yielded a return. I would begin to feel a new life rising within me. Through practice and exercise, I came to know that this life required an outlet, a form of projection or expression. As I tested out different forms I saw clearly that the arts offered the most potent resource for communion with loneliness and for self-renewal. Over a period of years I have tried many things. I have entered into free, unrestrained movement with jumps and leaps and twists and turns. I have moved into an open dance so completely that I would become absolutely exhausted. Yet within moments I would feel exhilarated, with limitless energy, boundlessness, and a sense of touching everything fully. Thus dance offered a crucial resource for living with loneliness. I also expressed myself through music, creating my own songs and listening to my own musical sounds. I actively sought the music of others learning that everyday music does not work for me in times of loneliness. It was necessary to listen to a music that had powerful shifts, valleys and peaks, unconnected sounds, the music of folk societies or Zen, Sufi, and Hasidism, music at the roots of people and culture, ethnic music that moved in spirals, that was unpredictable and strange, rather than standard music with its beginning, middle, and end, with its predictable melodies and outcomes.

Art experiences also worked, but only if they were completely unstructured—scribbling, doodling, sketching, marked shifts in textures and shadings, movement from subtle to bold colors, from dark to light. Whatever was spontaneous and in free form provided a source of meaning for lonely communication with myself, with nature, with life.

Sometimes I wrote in free style, in a stream-of-consciousness form, keeping a journal of these lonely encounters or a diary that was entirely spontaneous and uninhibited, written solely for myself without regard to rules or standards or anything that might be regarded as literary, purely self-expressive.

All these art forms at one time or another provided *the* medium for creative expression of loneliness. I have suggested them to others, in my teaching and therapy, in contacts with children and grown-ups. In each instance of resolution of the problem of loneliness, the people I have met and worked with have discovered their own process, the specific media through which they might learn to live with loneliness and to tap its source of energy and light, its potential for creative awareness and expression. It is often an "art" process in which there is a total shattering of old connections, a surrendering of one's self to a radical restructuring, and an assembling of a whole new set of feelings. The challenge of loneliness is to discover the creative process that fits a particular issue and offers expression and release, a new set of perceptions and the potentials for a new life.

I came to regard what I created in loneliness, the dramas and dialogues, the poems and songs, the new ways of being, as central features of my identity. It was in these lonely episodes that I learned what I had to offer in continuing to create a self. I came to feel free enough to invite others into my world of solitude, to share what I created, and to encourage and support others to find their own path, to enjoy its uniqueness, and appreciate its unpredictability.

Through loneliness, I have grown an identity that is unified, that remains strongly present in all of my encounters with life. At the core of my identity is a source of self-confirmation, often activated when I am not accepted, when others prefer me to be someone else. It is a solid place, nourished and supported by silence, solitude, and struggle. To be alive and to remain true to my own experiences, I have often wandered alone, to meditate, to search for an answer to suffering, rejection, and conflict. In times of crisis, I have found within myself a source of life that enables me to find a way to live. When everything else is in doubt, when I am unable to meet the requirements of life with others, I return to myself, to that lonely center of my life, and wait for new energy and new hope to be created. Alone, I search for perspectives and visions, for fresh connections, for a course that will affirm me, that will affirm others.

At such times, I experience shifts from solitude to loneliness not unlike that described by Nietzshe in *Thus Spake Zarathustra*:

> Oh Solitude! Solitude is my home. I have lived too long wildly in wild strange lands to come home to you without tears! . . .here you are at your own hearth and home; here you can utter everything and pour out every reason, nothing is here ashamed of hidden, hardened feelings.
>
> Here all things come caressingly to your discourse.
> Here you may speak to all things straight and true.
>
> But it is another thing to be lonely. For, do you remember, O Zarathustra? When once your bird cried above you as you stood in the forest undecided, ignorant where to go, beside a corpse.
>
> When you said: May my animals lead me! I found it more dangerous among men than among animals. *That* was loneliness!(1)

I have come to know the absolute necessity of moving off alone and finding special places for renewal of the life of silence. May Sarton speaks of a similar urgency in her *Journal Of A Solitude*:

> I am here alone for the first time in weeks, to take up my "real" life again at last. That is what is strange—that friends, even passionate love, are not my real life unless there is time alone in which to explore and to discover what

is happening or has happened. Without the interruptions, nourishing and maddening, this life would become arid. Yet I taste it fully only when I am alone here and "the house and I resume old conversations."(2)

Recently during one of these periods of solitude, the center of my world moved to Mary. I began to make contact with her current life, to feel her isolation. She is living in an important relationship, yet unable to share in a full way all that is vital inside, for no one person will ever fully meet and satisfy the inner requirements of another person, the multiple dimensions of being. In spite of the physical distance between us, I feel her sorrows, her anticipations of living, her dreams. As I struggle with this, a serious question emerges: Is there a tangible way to point to the expanded world within her reach, to offer her some new direction for life, an awareness of the promise of each day? If I were nearby I know I could infuse new energy into her world, new sources for valuing herself and staying in touch with what is uniquely her own. But we are apart, and I feel the agony of not being within reach. I stand alone in the darkness for a long time, staring into space, noticing the striking presence of the stars and the moon. In some strange way, the light from above enters my heart, and all at once my mood changes. I feel a definite hope and optimism. I am certain that I will find a way to help her create a life that will emphasize what she has always known with me, the unique, incomparable nature of her self, the feeling of being alive as an individual and being free to choose, to express, explore, and create in ways that respect, honor and affirm her as a precious human being. In this I know we are together, that we inspire each other, that the love and independence we have always known will continue to grow, that we will always be in touch, no matter how apart we are.

I experience a keen sense of tranquility as I settle peacefully in a comfortable chair. I am relaxed again and experiencing the joy of being alone. I sit quietly and feel the wonder of silence. After a while, my mood changes, and my friend Dorothy comes clearly into view. I have just learned that she is in the final hours of her life. I am wanting to be with her now, to feel something of what she is facing at this moment. I am aware of the pain of her illness, and my tears begin to flow freely. I enter fully into this moment, shutting off all other visions and sounds. I imagine her last hours of farewell with friends and members of her family. I am aware of how hard it is to bring a relationship to a close, and simultaneously aware that what I have shared with Dorothy will always live within me. These moments of farewell pass before me and for a while I experience the joy of what we have created—our dialogues that always inspired, our deep faith in each other, our unconditional love.

A few hours later, I learn of Dorothy's death. I move quickly to my private sanctuary near the woods and steep myself in the life we have known. I feel her tangible presence and my words begin to flow out to her:

Dorothy, I wish I knew how to let go gently, how to be ready, how to have prepared myself for your death. I know you suffered in your valiant struggle for life these past months. You transcended the pain and horror long enough to say a closing farewell to all the places and people you loved in Yelping Hill, in Greece, in Israel, and then you came home to die in Cambridge. You fulfilled the promise of life in taking leave of all the worlds in which your deepest roots were growing. There were times when it hurt deeply to listen to the rasping quality of your voice, when it diminished noticeably until even your saliva was gone and you were absolutely silenced.

In these last months your letters and cassettes came to me with a special spark. Unbelievably, at times you managed to some degree to retain the power of your own self, to affirm your being and declare your intentions and convictions—in spite of the ravaging disease, the loss of memory and all the other horrors. The suddenness of your energy was always a great surprise. You spoke to me in the language of love. And together we kept our faith in each other alive, glowing to the last moments and we put the finishing touches on your book, *Valuing The Self*.(3) What had you said, that you did not need or want to publish at all, that *Freedom and Culture* had fixed you and you were determined not to be fossilized again.(4) And then the whirlwind had started. People writing to say how your writings and talks had changed their lives, how they were able to immerse themselves in root meanings that often moved them in spirals, rather than straight lines, and brought a new depth and richness to their living. But what finally triggered your decision to publish was the realization that you would be leaving your papers and notes behind and that someone you loved would then be responsible for deciding what to do with them. And that was not you, Dorothy—ever—to let someone else take responsibility for your fate, do for you what you were capable of doing for yourself. You had a choice, as you put it, to burn all your papers and transcripts of your talks or to work with them and publish them as a book. I'm glad you chose to create this final manuscript, though you knew I would have understood and accepted whatever decision you made.

I feel an urgency to speak to you on this day of your death. I want to let go of all the earthly things—your voice, full, deep, warm, with its energy and power and devotion;

your face that expressed openly and distinctly all your ranging moods and feelings; your touch that awakened everything around you; your body so fully alive, so clearly present; and your spirit that filled the rooms you walked in. I am hanging onto all of this now. Yet even while I feel the fullness of the life we shared I know that I will let go, that you will merge with everything that is vital in my life, with the wind and the trees, the hills, and the flowers that you held so dearly. I know in time that you will be a natural part of all that is alive in me, unified where my roots grow, where the bonds of love are permanent and indelible.

I have known your unique being and cherished the way we were together. I've suffered and struggled with you in battles with the establishment when the odds were against us. I've known the fullness of your laughter, the stories and songs you inspired, your way of bringing life to an idea, your valuing of truth and beauty in nature, and all that is human in living and dying.

I am with the mystery of the living spirit that follows death, with you in everyday memories and dreams, knowing that what we created remains in gentle graces, in human communion, wherever love exists.

Sometimes only as death approaches is the value of intimate contact with others fully realized. Then, there is an appeal to know people in compassionate, direct human ways. There is often a reaching out for what matters most in life with others. This letter written to nurses by a student nurse dying of cancer strongly calls out for sensitive touch and caring in the critical moments of dying.

I am a student nurse. I am dying. I write this to you who are, and will become, nurses in the hope that by my sharing my feelings with you, you may someday be better able to help those who share my experience. . . . Nursing must be advancing, but I wish it would hurry. We're taught not to be overly cheery now, to omit the "Everything's fine" routine, and we have done pretty well. But now one is left in a lonely silent void. With the protective "fine, fine" gone, the staff is left with only their own vulnerability and fear. The dying patient is not yet seen as a person and thus cannot be communicated with as such. He is a symbol of what every human fears and what we each know, at least academically, that we too must someday face. . . .

But for me, fear is today and dying is now. You slip in and out of my room, give me medications and check my blood pressure. Is it because I am a student nurse myself, or just a human being, that I sense your fright? And your fears enhance mine. Why are you afraid? I am the one who is dying!

I know you feel insecure, don't know what to say, don't know what to do. But please believe me, if you care, you can't go wrong. Don't run away—wait—all I want to know is that there will be someone to hold my hand when I need it. I am afraid. Death may get to be a routine to you, but it is new to me. You may not see me as unique, but I've never died before.

You whisper about my youth, but when one is dying, is he really so young anymore? I have lots I wish we could talk about. It really would not take much more of your time because you are in here quite a bit anyway.

If only we could be honest, both admit of our fears, touch one another. If you really care, would you lose so much of your valuable professionalism if you even cried with me? Just person to person? Then, it might not be so hard to die—in a hospital.(5)

In a very real sense the question of being or nonbeing,

of living or dying, is faced again and again in the crises and turning points that are a part of every life. Within this struggle is the challenge to remain alive as a unique and independent self while at the same time relating with others in an open and authentic way.

Loneliness is a universal phenomenon, the inevitable outcome of the human condition. Rudimentary feelings of loneliness are experienced from the beginning of life and reach a peak in awareness during adolescence and again in old age. Feelings of loneliness are especially marked during periods of transition, during times of illness, tragedy and death, and as a response to failures to be and grow as a self and to fulfill one's potentials as a particular individual. Pain and suffering are inevitable during these moments of facing the challenges of living and dying. The search for an answer or a way to continue to live and the agony of conflict and terror severely threaten the sense of self, the meaning of life, and the value of existence itself.

I first began to discover the roots of my own loneliness during a family crisis when all roads to other people ended, when nothing or no one could reach or soften the searing pain in my heart. The sense of being clearly apart from others plunged me forcefully into my own self and brought to my awareness the stark reality of what it means to be an utterly lonely person. In those hours and days, there was danger that I would sink into total despair. Fortunately, I began to realize that it was my rejection of loneliness and my running away from it that put me in a state of depression. When I accepted myself as a lonely person, when I learned to stay with my feelings of being separate and apart, when I internalized these feelings as an ultimate reality, as something intense and total, beyond communication or understanding, then I began to breathe fully and freely. In solitary encounters with nature, I realized that I would never again see the sun fading into oblivion without a sense of loneliness. I would never again witness alienation and broken human moments without being deeply and sharply affected. The recognition of my own basic loneliness opened a wide range of awarenesses and feelings. As I focused inwardly, my world expanded, my relationships with others deepened. Something powerful took root in me. I began to create life in many new directions and to flourish as an individual. Ideas, images, feelings came freely. I found a way to let these painful awakenings flow in written form; I began to talk honestly and completely with myself. All of the important relationships in my life became more profoundly personal and human. A pattern was established for communicating with nature, with others, with myself; and that pattern has been fulfilled in many different worlds. I have learned to live alone, to respect my own inner life, to pursue my own sense of direction.

I have learned to be with others in utter silence, in wide ranges of color, texture, and movement, taking the path of the heart, trusting invisible messages.

I have learned to infuse my spirit into each human venture, to risk myself in the hope of knowing the glory of a voice that speaks for the first time, of witnessing the birth of individuality, of seeing energy and spirit suddenly merging into new activities and forms, of sparking and sustaining a light from within that continues to glow even in darkness.

In loneliness I have discovered a way to be creative, losing myself as a separate person yet remaining absolutely connected to the moment, in writing, in movement and dance, in music, in ideas, or in silence. I have learned to let go of everything external and extraneous, of everything purposive and controlling, to permit the most distinctive awarenesses of the moment to shine forth, to base reality on my own senses, to see and hear in totally distinctive ways.

When creativity is pursued in loneliness all of one's energy and spirit enters the moment. Being creative means being solitary, facing the unknown, and experiencing an unpredictable process, with focus, concentration, and exertion, in which there is an unfolding of one's own self, exploring, experimenting, moving towards new ways of being and becoming.

Sometimes the habits and patterns between children and parents remain set regardless of change and upheaval in life. In these relationships there often is a real hungering, a yearning for deeper connections. Perhaps there will always be an awareness of the loneliness of not having fully met persons with whom we share the everyday physical world, meals and furnishings, offices and homes. In her biography, *Sido*, Colette portrays the hungering gaps in her relationship with her father.

> It seems strange to me, now, that I knew him so little. . . . I could go straight to the corner of our garden where the snowdrops bloomed. And I could paint from memory the climbing rose, and the trellis that supported it, as well as the hole in the wall and the worn flagstone. . . . But elsewhere he is a wandering, floating figure, full of gaps, obscured by clouds and only visible in patches. . . . Too late, too late. That is always the cry of children, of the negligent and the ungrateful. Not that I consider myself more guilty than any other "child," on the contrary. But while he was alive, ought I not to have seen through his humorous dignity and his feigned frivolity? Were we not worthy, he and I, of a mutual effort to know each other better?(6)

Sometimes it is only in the depths of loneliness that an awakening occurs, and old attitudes and ways are suddenly dropped in favor of a new perspective. Sheldon Kopp, writing of his constant battle to overcome his shyness, powerfully describes the process in the following passage:

> . . . this time I smoked in turn because this magic time would be different. After a bit I was high. It was good and I was filled with nostalgia, but it didn't do it. Being high had never let me go anywhere alone with anyone else. . . .
>
> That was when I finally got to it. This is just the way it was going to be. I could lose fifty pounds and be beautiful. I could write my Book of Books, and have it an underground success. I could even die and be reborn. But no matter what, I would always be as painfully shy and as bewildered by the social talk that brings people together, as shy and as bewildered as I had been since I was a kid. Without knowing what you say to leave without hurting, I pushed back my chair, stood up awkwardly, and silently wandered away.
>
> When I awoke I knew, for the first time that. . . The shyness is mine, like it or not. It's the best of me and the worst of me, and only the covering it up, the hiding it, and the running from it is not me.(7)

Another kind of loneliness grows out of the struggle to relate with a person who does not respond. The challenge is to remain alive in that relationship, to continue impinging on that person, continue to hope that eventually there will be recognition and dialogue. Persistence and determination may keep one on the path of the other but this is often a frustrating and discouraging time. This was the experience of a young therapist who had struggled for months to awaken a child to the potentials of relationship and finally caught a fleeting glimpse of what it is like, enough to nourish and sustain his belief in the future.

So many times you have stood on trembling legs, your entire body jerking. I felt big and bad.

So many times you cried and choked. I sensed the helplessness and fear in those moments.

I took you into my arms but you remained rigid. I too felt afraid.

At our next meeting I sat apart from you. As our time drew to a close you ever so slowly crossed the room, eyes fixed on the floor. You moved into my waiting arms and we were together, truly together for the first time. My heart sang.

Then in our last meeting, as if starting anew, you sat with your back to me. I was hurt. Then you turned and our eyes met. Your eyes spoke to me, asking me to "wait, please wait."

Keri, I wait for you and I know you will come.(8)

An illustration of a similar struggle between child and adult follows:

You are a little quieter today. But you grab my hand as always. I am still a little lost in my own thoughts. I have not yet become fully aware of you beside me, of your silence, of the heaviness of your steps.

As I begin to notice you, slowly it creeps up on me. Your sadness is so present that it seems to seep through every movement of your body, every pore of your expression. My God, you overwhelm me. I am at a loss for words or actions that might ease the weight I see upon your shoulders. I stand awkward before you. desperately wanting to find some way to rid you of your pain.

But I am forced to wait. I sit back and push the frantic thinking from my mind. You will let me know in time. You will show me how I might be with you.

Slowly, oh slowly, you turn furtively to check if I am present. Again you turn, and again, and again. When you are ready, when you can allow me into your world, you creep closer. It is not quite enough though, so you climb into my lap and snuggle beneath my chin.

My awkwardness and waiting subside. I am free now to give myself to you. You have shown me a way to be with you. I hold you and rock you and sing sweet lullabies. Your body relaxes, your expression of strain eases and you fall asleep.(9)

The acceptance and valuing of one's own self in times of loneliness is a way of being in touch with the growing and becoming potentials that are within. At such times the real nature of life often reveals itself. Utterly alone and desolate, one finally reaches the critical truth. Pushed to the brink, at the extremes of living and dying, at last the individual comes to a shocking awareness that alters the entire course of life. Nothing or no one but the person can find the way out. The decision to live honestly is sometimes reached at the end of a diminishing and defeating relationship.

In his book *How People Change*, Wheelis describes his relationship with his father, a powerful, controlling man who attempted in every conversation to mold and shape him into a competitive, industrious successful scientist. His father's tactics included manipulating questions, diminishing accusations, use of labels like stupid and lazy, and the frequent branding of him as a selfish person and a liar, a "low-down, no-account scoundrel."

Throughout his life he had actively fought against these labels, yet they continued to plague him and affect his life. Whereas poetry or paintings otherwise might have become a central focus, he withdrew, for nothing he created ever reached that level of perfection that was acceptable. One day on the brink of disaster, painfully apart and isolated, for the first time he spoke with powerful words to his now-dead father. He declared his independence and washed away the poisons that imprisoned him and the voice that constantly hovered over him.

When next I feel those steel fingers close around my heart I must seek a division of self, must find a way of turning around inside, as it were, to discover those pale blue eyes still fixed upon me, and to reject at last the ancient accusation, must face my father who now is the condemning part of self, and say, "It is *you* who are the enemy, not those out there. It is *you* who would destroy me!"

Anger is what I need. To cringe before that inner denunciation is to perpetuate the past, to reaffirm my father's authority to determine how I regard myself. All these years his judgment has held sway; now I must find a way, without tearing the whole house down, to rise up against him, to seek him out who now is part of me, who still wordlessly condemns me as unworthy. If I have something to say and mean it I must stand behind it, must mobilize a dark and deep-running anger to protect it.(10)

In creative loneliness, there is a determination to be. New feelings arise, dreams and memories, desires, and imaginings. There is often a sense of the eternal rhythms of life, a special awareness and connection with nature. Leaves and grass, earth and sky become strikingly vivid, gentle callings, whisperings to sense and feel the significance of universal ties, of the mysterious connections to color, movement, texture, and pattern, to know the meaning of life and recognize the pervasive fullness in being alive now.

My encounters with loneliness have awakened within me the desire to know life with others fully, in silence and in dialogue, intuitively to feel, to sense, to enter into the timeless rhythms, attuned to create what is essential, what is whole, what is uniquely mine and yours. Before I enter a new situation, before I meet a new person, I take time to be quietly alone, to anticipate this new life I am about to begin. I become aware in my solitude of the particularity of each relationship. I want to experience the unique rhythms, the ranges and extremes, and the steady unfolding, the full potential of life with each person, stretching and moving forward in a life that is mutual but that at the same time recognizes the inevitability of privacy, individuality, and separateness. I want to participate in the concrete unfolding, in the mystery of human engagement, and in the incomprehensible nature of the true life between myself and others.

Mike entered on that first day of therapy—proud, strikingly present, alive in exuberant, quick movements. From the start he knew what he wanted to do. It was clear that he would not be dominated by anyone. He stood up for himself and let others know quickly that he was in charge of his life. There were times in his sessions with Barry when Barry tried to direct him, but Mike always held his ground and moved in a determined and independent way. If his themes of play and conversation were indicative, Mike was screaming with his body. He was at war with the world, a strong voice crying out: "I am! I am! I am!"

One group of items Mike used expressed his angry feelings—bows and arrows, dart gun, knives, and Bobo, the comeback clown that he regularly battered, slashed, squeezed and crushed. But Mike also was entranced with the castanets, the tom-toms, the xylophone, and the flute. Using play materials as weapons, Mike established a series of scenes devastating in their form of destructiveness. He easily decapitated human figures. Drownings, strangulations, shooting people with darts and arrows from different heights, smothering with sand, and a variety of other tortures were ways for expressing anger and rejection, his response to efforts of grown-ups to keep him in prison. He knew the rights of children and who in our society violates these rights. In Mike's role-playing and dramas he clearly named the argumentative, belligerent, continually battling puppets. And the battles went on and on until Mike interjected loud, piercing screams and terminated the fighting by pulling the puppets apart, out of the playhouse, down the rooftop, and Bang! Crash! onto the surface below.

Interwoven with the aggressive dramas was Mike's solitary fascination with music. He enjoyed playing several instruments at once, listening to single sounds, experimenting with different combinations, and suddenly it would all come together. His face would light up and he would play with a rhythm and a gusto. At such times he would look at me with eyes aglow.

Yes, Mike, it is something to create what is truly your own. Nothing else will ever give that kind of inner ecstasy, to participate freely and fully in the making of your own creation. I am glad we met and you came to know that not all grown-ups want to fetter you and keep you down. I'm glad I helped you feel what it is like to be recognized and affirmed, for you not to have to seek my regard but to have it as a pure and unconditional gift. I am glad that I was witness to those lively rhythms, that I saw your spirit live and grow. I'm glad I experienced with you the light of creation and the joy in your heart.(11)

Increasingly, I am discovering that when I am truly ready to feel, to hear, to see what is before me and in me, to be responsive to my own senses and intuitions, when I am ready to flow through my own inner life into the unfolding life of the other, unusual events occur; life moves into new experiences and activities. The essence of creative life with others is rooted in the fact that each person has a share in the other, a commitment and involvement, each is willing to risk and challenge, to push and be pushed, to be firm and angry, to be soft and tender, to be and to grow. To meet life as it is means to trust in the mystery of each experience and to permit the unknown and unpredictable to guide the process. When we are fully present and responsive with ourselves and with others, life becomes a continual awakening and the persons involved enter into an unknown and unpredictable journey. We honor life by recognizing it as it is and by creating new life.(12) This inevitably means that, at times, we will choose the path of loneliness, for it is the way to a new beginning, new hope, new awareness, a resurgence of energy and vitality. We may have to descend into the forces of darkness that pull us to earth and weigh us down, in order to experience new visions of life with others, in order to feel joy and fly again.

REFERENCES

1. NIETZSCHE, FRIEDRICH. *Thus Spake Zarathustra*. Tr. by R. J. Hollingdale. Baltimore: Penguin Books, 1961, pp. 202–203.

2. SARTON, MAY. *Journal of A Solitude*. New York: W.W. Norton & Co., Inc. 1973, p. 11.

3. LEE, DOROTHY. *Valuing The Self*. Englewood Cliffs, N.J.: Prentice-Hall, 1976.

4. LEE, DOROTHY. *Freedom and Culture*. Englewood Cliffs, N.J.: Prentice-Hall, 1959.

5. ANONYMOUS. "Death in the First Person." *Amer. J. of Nursing*, Vol. 70, No. 2, February, 1970, p. 336.

6. COLETTE. *My Mother's House and Sido*. New York: Farrar, Straus and Young, Inc., 1953, pp. 175–181.

7. KOPP, SHELDON. *If You Meet the Buddha on the Road, Kill Him!* Palo Alto, Calif.: Science and Behavior Books, Inc., 1972, p. 164.

8. HERRINGTON, JOSEPH, JR. Personal Communication, January, 1976.

9. HODDINOTT, PEG. "The Growing Edge." Unpublished manuscript, The Merrill-Palmer Institute, 1976.

10. WHEELIS, ALAN. *How People Change.* New York: Harper and Row, 1973, pp. 32–33.

11. MOUSTAKAS, CLARK. *Who Will Listen?* New York: Ballantine, 1975, pp. 51–53.

12. MOUSTAKAS, CLARK. *Ibid.*, p. 133.